To those whose voices are silenced:
May one day your story be heard.

UNHEARD
a memoir

BY
SUSANNA HARTIGAN

An Abstract Lucidity Publication

AP

This book is a memoir based on the author's memory and told from a child's point of view. Time sequences and dialogue may be generalized, but events are true. Some names, locations, and details have been changed for identity purposes.

No part of this publication may be copied without written permission of the author or publisher except for brief quotations of printed reviews. Unauthorized reproduction of this copyrighted work is illegal. Participation in electronic piracy of this material is punishable by law.

Library of Congress Cataloguing in Publication Data
Library of Congress Control Number: 2010915327

UNHEARD

Copyright ©2010 Susanna Hartigan

All Rights Reserved

http://susannahartigan.blogspot.com

Printed in the United States of America

ISBN - 978-0-615-42171-1

First Edition

Edited by Susanna Hartigan

Published by Abstract Lucidity, PO Box 1255, Edgewater, FL 32141

Cover Design by Abstract Lucidity

Cover Photos Copyright ©2010 Abstract Lucidity

http://abstractlucidity.zenfolio.com

Chapter One
Him

As soon as I hear the weight of his body touch the first step, I silently but quickly scamper back to my bed, crawl under the covers, and pretend to be asleep. My heart pounding in my chest like a jackhammer, I pray he doesn't hear me or open my door. I hear his foot reach the third step from the top, the one that annoyingly creaks when anyone touches it, and my body tenses even more. It is difficult to breathe noiselessly, but by now I am used to trying my best to be unheard.

The split second it takes him to reach the top of the stairs and make his way to the bathroom seems like an eternity. I hear the bathroom door shut and feel a sigh of relief; I can breathe again, at least for a short time. I lay watching the second-hand of my electric clock rotate its face. I listen to the clink of the toilet seat hit the cover, the waterfall of beer-urine hitting the toilet water, and the old pipes sucking it all up when the toilet flushes.

Then I hear the elephant. The elephant, as I call it, is the loud air in the old pipes when the sink or shower water runs to the second floor. The elephant stops, and I tense again, knowing he will be coming back out and wondering if he will go back downstairs. Or will he do what he often does and stand in front of my door listening for me to make a wrong move?

The bathroom door opens so quickly it startles me, and I almost gasp for air loud enough to be heard. I watch for his feet near my door, listening intently to determine where he is going. I don't think he knows I can feel his negative presence on the other side of my door - nor does he realize that I can see the reflection of his feet on the wooden floor. Although they are mostly unexpected, I am aware of his games, and I am not about to let him beat me. I have to be sure that in order to survive his mind games, I need to be two steps ahead of him.

Hearing the third step creak, I breathe a sigh of relief that I am once again alone upstairs. I reach for the book underneath my pillow and go back to my window to continue reading in the light. Having to go to bed at 7 p.m. at the age of eleven is humiliating, but I am used to dealing with these ridiculous punishments over minor infractions. I escape this home prison by going to school during the day and by reading books at night. It is the only way I manage to keep sane.

The sun goes down. I have no way to see what I am reading, but during the Florida summer months, I can grab enough light until about 8:30 p.m. Daddy knows about the situation, and I use a small flashlight he gave me. I do my best not to get caught with it.

Morning comes quickly, and I look forward to going to school. The only bad part is that I have to sit next to him in the car on the way there. At 6:30 a.m., we get in the little blue car and he promptly pops open a can of beer and drinks it on my way to school, he on his way to work.

The ten-mile drive consists of silence. Sketchy eyes peering at me from the corners, listening to the sipping of his beer, I cannot wait to get to school. There is no morning radio, and communication is nonexistent. We arrive at my school, and as usual, I get out of the car, say goodbye, barely getting an utter in return. I must also say, "Thank you," or face the consequences, since he considers driving me to school a favor, even though I have no other way to get here.

I arrive at school earlier than everyone else, since our new place is further than any buses are zoned, and he has to be to work early. I wait for my friend Cindy, walk to the store to look at magazines, then walk the block back to school before the bell rings. I go about my day at school, listening to my new teacher read aloud George Orwell's "1984", and still try to fit in with the new class. Unlike them, I dread when the school bell rings at the end of the day.

*   *   *   *   *

I miss our old house. Well, maybe not the house itself but its location. I had friends in my old neighborhood, my grandparents, my great grandma and great aunts - all within walking distance. A few blocks from my old house were ducks at the canal that I fed stale bread to while trying to run from them as they tried to attack me. Around the corner was my favorite Jiffy Store where I'd stand for hours playing Space Invaders at the arcade machine, buying candy cigarettes, and talking to the friendly clerks that all knew me by name. They knew me because they knew him, and he had been sending me there to buy his Winstons since I was eight.

I used to ride my bike for miles all within a one-mile radius and felt as if I'd encircled the entire world. Sometimes I'd sneak to see my friends in the other neighborhood - the one by the river. Most of my friends lived within a street away from each other. Allison lives with her grandmother because her mother has too many kids and couldn't take care of her. Jessica's parents are always at work, and the new girl, Danielle, lives with her divorced mother. Fabia and Fran both have strict parents but still manage to be able to do fun things.

I had two friends nearby that I saw after school when I was allowed. One was Carly, whose grandparents lived in a trailer. She and her older sister visited their grandparents after school until their working parents came to pick them up. Carly wasn't one of the friends that I looked forward to being with because she seemed immature and a crybaby much of the time, but it was better than being at my house while he was home was more pleasurable.

Another friend a few streets away was Rebekah. Even though her parents were very strict Mormons and she wasn't allowed to play outside much, we had a lot of fun together at her house. Rebekah was never allowed at my house, and I stopped going to hers when I was ten because her father kept making me sit on his lap, facing and straddling him as he held me close. He gave me the creeps. When I tried to scoot away he forcefully continued to pull me forward. He also liked to hug me a lot, which I also thought was creepy. I wasn't used to hugs much from home, but I knew that my grandparents never hugged me like that. I knew in my stomach that something was wrong about it.

*   *   *   *   *

I can't do any of the fun stuff at the new house. I have no friends, no family within walking distance, no ducks to feed, and nowhere safe to ride a bike. The closest convenience store parking lot is laced with crack dealers and hookers, like the rest of the neighborhood. The one time I did ride my bike a few blocks away, I witnessed an elderly woman getting robbed in the IGA grocery store parking lot. Hearing the woman yell and scream that the man on the bike had taken her money for the month made me realize I shouldn't be down there by myself anymore.

The new house is old – the plumbing croaks, the floors creak, and the walls and floors both crawl – literally – with cockroaches at night. It isn't because we're dirty people. My mother is one of the best and most consistent housekeepers around; she dusts and vacuums daily, if not twice daily. Despite my mother's cleanliness, nothing seems to help the home that reeks of poverty. It's the way it is in old Florida homes run by slumlords.

Palmetto bugs are known to fly out of the trees and into your face when you open the door at night, making their way into the house to hide and breed. Termites are feasting on the wooden floors under the ugly carpet, revealed one day when one of us stepped into a hole in the kitchen.

Besides the house being old it is plain ugly, and it *smells* old. The odor of old rotting wood, mildew and mold permeates the house. The humidity, especially in the summer, brings the odor to its ripest scent; the rain tops it off.

The kitchen has flat brown carpet with orange specks, and the living room has an olive and sea foam green colored mix of shag carpet. Dull, light green paint lines the walls along the stairway, while the rest of the inside of the house is either flat white or beige, the paint mostly old and cracked. The outside of the house has chipped white paint, as well as the wooden roach-infested garage in the back. Like the rest of the sidewalks in the area, the front walkway is cracked and crooked.

All of the appliances and fixtures are old – the sinks require special ways to turn off the water or it continues running, and the hot water only lasts a few short minutes. The stove has to be lit with a match, and since there is no air conditioning, summers are brutal. Winters aren't much better with the only heater being downstairs and blankets being scarce. Sometimes we are lucky enough to borrow space heaters.

"This house is haunted," my mother says. "Someone was walking up and down the steps last night, and it wasn't any of us."

I have never witnessed anything ghostly in the house myself, but the place has its own set of living haunts.

Considering I spend a lot of time in it, my new room is a blessing compared to the four-by-six-foot one I had at the old trailer house until the babies were born. After that, I moved into a larger bedroom in the trailer, but I hated having to listen to his brother having sex or arguing with his new teenage wife.

The new room is much larger than I am used to, with wooden floors and two long windows. One window faces the house with dirty bikers next door, while the other window faces the street, the one where I spend most of my time reading and observing the neighbors across the street. Our standard of life has certainly changed since *he* came along.

* * * * *

The only reason I look forward to going home is to see the babies. I love taking them for walks up and down the sidewalk in their twin stroller. I love being the big sister, and I love that walking them gets me out of the house in hopes of meeting some friends.

I finally meet the neighbors across the street. It is a grandmother and her grandchildren, and some guy who rents the apartment behind them whom I nicknamed "Scaggly" because of his appearance. He wears cut off shorts and no shirt. His unkempt hair is down to his shoulders, and he drives a loud Trans Am. But he is nice to me, and I have a crush on Scaggly because I am lonely. When I sit at my window each night, I watch him come and go and hope to see him before it gets too late and I have to go to sleep. I secretly wish Scaggly would take me away from here.

Sometimes on walks I pass people, usually senior citizens. They stop to look at the babies and ask if they are mine. Even though I am only eleven, I look older.

Walking the babies has become one of my chores, and now he makes me walk them before I am allowed to do my homework. I bring a book with me to read as I push them along. He sees that I am enjoying my reading and walking sessions and tells me I am not allowed to walk the babies with a book in my hand.

"You might run into a car," he barks.

"On the sidewalk?" I question.

"It doesn't matter. No more books."

The house is not a home when he is there. Fear lingers in the air, and even my mother is a very different person with him around. She does everything to please him and make him happy at everyone else's expense including her own. The few times in her life that she stood up for me ended in an ensuing all-night battle, as with anything else minor that sets him off.

I am not always what they fight about. He nit picks at everything. Ever since she's been with him he fights with her over things that are irrelevant to the rest of the world. He argues with her all night long if a man looks at her. He accuses her of thinking things about him that he probably thinks about himself. Much of the time he doesn't make any sense at all. He feels that she doesn't give him enough love, and I spend many nights lying in bed, listening to hours of endless yelling, arguing, nonsensical questions, and abjurations.

"Love on me," he whines, sounding like a desperate, four-year-old.

I can hear my mother's anguish in her sighs as I suppose she tries to love on him, whatever that means. A few minutes later he says it again. And hours later I hear him saying it again and again, over and over, and they fight until the early morning about why she won't love on him.

"I'm *sick* of loving on you!" I finally hear her yell back.

There are many mornings she wakes up with bruises on her arms and wrists from his grabbing and pushing her around;

she is exhausted because he didn't allow her to sleep until she showed him love.

I dare not allow him to know that I am awake through it all, hearing every sound. Even if I have to get up to use the bathroom he croaks, "Get back in bed!" as if it is normal to be able to sleep through such a racket. Any noise that I make immediately alerts his attention and I hear him snarl my name as if I am the most disgusting thing on the planet.

No matter what I do, I always feel as if I am walking in a land mine-filled area - one wrong move and I am dead meat. There are times when I actually do fear that he will kill me, because I can feel his hatred burn into my soul whenever he speaks or looks at me with his shifty eyes. I can see him watch me out of the corner of his eyes when I walk into a room, as if he is trying to catch me doing something. Oddly, he never looks me *in* the eye.

Hearing him speak makes me cringe. My shoulders curl inward, my throat tightens, and my heart palpitates. My stomach remains in a steady knot much of the time, making it difficult to eat. Picking is the one thing that helps me keep my focus off of him.

He accuses me of things I don't do and makes up lies to tell Mom so he can punish me. When I squint my eyes, he accuses me of giving him dirty looks, even if I am twenty feet away. When I take a deep breath, he accuses me of being sarcastic, even though there is no conversation. He accuses me of smacking my food on top of my mouth when I eat – even if I am aware of how I am eating and consciously make an effort to make no noise. If I make one sound when I walk he accuses me of stomping my feet, even though I consciously tiptoe. Still, *he* can hear it because he wants to hear it. If there is no sound, he makes it up in his mind. No one is allowed to believe anything I say because he doesn't allow it. If Mom says anything to him in disagreement, he convinces her that she is wrong, and eventually she believes him. No matter how hard I try, I cannot do anything right.

I consider throwing myself out of the second story window, but I figure I'll end up crippling myself and get in even more trouble. I want to either die or get out of here, and I know that it will be soon before at least one of them happens. I am willing to do anything to get away from *him*.

Chapter Two
Before Him

Mommy and Daddy had me during the summer after they got out of high school, but not before Papa made them get married when they found out Mommy was pregnant. We lived in a yellow house with a big yard on the corner of two streets, where Mommy said I ate roly-poly bugs while she hanged laundry or mowed the lawn in the sun. Daddy came home from working in the fields every day saying he was tired, and every day he lay down on the living room floor for his hurt back. One time I made him mad by circling him around and around, pretending that I was going to stick my big toe in his eye.

"Don't you stick your toe in my eye," he warned.

I thought it would be funny to do it anyway, so I did. He spanked me, and I never stuck my big toe in his eye again.

Another time I made Daddy mad was when I woke up in my crib and cried for water in the middle of the night. He brought me a glass with Ronald McDonald on it filled with water. I sipped.

"Here, drink more," he demanded.

"No," I cried, still half asleep.

He threw the rest of it in my face. I screamed like the baby I was; he wiped me up with one of Mommy's kitchen towels.

Mommy and Daddy worked a lot, and for a while Mommy went to school to be a nurse. Daddy bought a boat and they argued over money. On weekends we went on the river to the island with their friends. Daddy liked taking pictures, so he had Mommy and me model for him on the island. We stood on the big trees that washed up from the storm. I looked at him and smiled but Mommy never smiled. She wasn't happy with the way she looked, even though everyone told her that she looked like Farrah Fawcett.

*   *   *   *   *

Summertime in Florida means a lot of thunderstorms. There was a really big storm called Hurricane David, and we had a big party at our house. At first it was only supposed to be a vacation for my grandparents and aunts because they all lived in mobile homes at the old people's park near us. But it turned out that they invited all of their friends and neighbors, too. All of the old people were crammed into our small apartment all night until the hurricane left. I didn't know that old people could be so loud, especially the old ladies, because they were drinking a lot of beer and wine. Not even the thunder and rain could drown out the chatter and laughter.

After the hurricane was Halloween. Mommy made my costumes every year. One time she sewed up a clown suit, dyed one side red and the other side blue, then did the same to a mop for me to wear as a wig and painted up my face up like a clown. She and Daddy took me to a burger place and entered me in a contest. It was hot, and I had to stand around a bunch of adults dressed weird.

Then I heard the man announce, "And the winner is… number 41, the clown!"

I won first place! My prize was twenty silver dollars. I didn't know what that meant, but Mommy and Daddy said it was a lot of money.

On another Halloween, Mommy dressed me in torn sheets and wrapped me up as a mummy, but I only got about halfway around the block before the sheets started unraveling. She fixed them, but they came off anyway. We didn't have another costume, so Mommy gave me her black bathing suit and tied it up so that it fit my body. She stuffed the top with socks to give me bumps, and she put a bunch of her makeup on my face and some high heels to wear. I liked wearing Mommy's clothes but I didn't know what to tell people I was when they asked me.

"Tell them you're a sex symbol," she giggled.

I didn't know what the words *sex* or *symbol* meant, but I knew they must have been something important if only adults knew about it.

I marched right up to a neighbor's house and yelled "Trick or treat!" until a middle-aged couple answered their door.

"What are you supposed to be?" the lady asked me.

"A sex symbol," I proudly said with bright red lipstick all over my lips and dark pink blush on my cheeks.

When the lady's eyes got big, and the couple gave each other funny looks, I guessed that a sex symbol probably wasn't something that a seven-year-old girl was supposed to be on Halloween.

* * * * *

During the weekdays I stayed with Gramma and Papa while Mommy and Daddy worked. Mommy was a nurse and had to leave very early in the morning in her white uniform, nurse's hat and silver name tag. At first she worked with babies at the hospital, but then she worked for the electric company taking care of people that got hurt. Daddy still worked in the fields and swamps, and he came home dirty.

I spent a lot of time at Gramma and Papa's house on the weekends. Sometimes Mommy got all dressed up, looking really pretty in her red or flowery black dresses, her red heart necklace, makeup, and winged hair to go out dancing with her friends. Daddy got all dressed up to go out in his collared shirt and cologne, but it didn't seem like they went out together much.

If I didn't stay at Gramma and Papa's, I stayed home with a teenaged babysitter named Maxine. At first I liked Maxine, but then she got mean. She wouldn't let me watch TV because she wanted to listen to music. When I stood in front of the TV she yelled at me to get out of her way, because she liked to put on bikinis, look at her reflection in the TV, and dance around. Then she made me go to bed. I told Mommy about Maxine's bikinis in front of the TV. She never came to babysit me again.

One night Mommy took me to her friend Sheila's. Sheila lived in a small trailer in a park with lots of other trailers and loud people and dirty kids. The road was dirty and small and the cars were ugly and rusted up. Their house was dark inside, but my favorite part was the beads that Sheila hung in the doorway. I played in them - walking through them back and forth, pretending the beads were my long hair.

Sheila's teenage son, Brian, babysat me when Mommy and Sheila left to go out for the night. After watching some TV on the living room floor, Brian came out of his room, unbuttoned his pants and showed me his privates. I'd never seen a boy's privates before except maybe when I watched someone change a baby diaper. He told me since he showed me his, it was my turn to show him mine. I didn't want to. I was embarrassed. He got mad at me and made me go into his messy room. There were clothes all over the floor and a toy basketball hoop. He unbuttoned my pale red shorts and broke the button off of them, telling me to tell Mommy that it happened when I went to the bathroom. Then he told me to lie down on his bed.

He put his mouth on me down there and said, "Doesn't that feel good?"

I didn't like it but I told him "Uh huh," because I didn't want to make him mad again. I thought it was gross, and why would someone put his mouth where I pee?

He still had his pants down, and when he kept getting up to look out the window to see if our moms were home, I could see gross red bumps all over his bum. When Brian was done he told me that I had to do the same to him. All I could think was that's where pee comes from, and I don't want to put my mouth on pee. I told him no, I don't want to do it. He told me I had to do it because he did it to me. I almost threw up but I did it for a few seconds. He told me to do it more. I said no more. He got mad and said he was going to stick it in me. I didn't know you could stick something in down there. I don't think he ever got it in but he poked around for a while, and I was all red and sore afterwards.

I went into the living room and fell asleep watching TV. Mommy must have picked me up late because I don't remember her coming to get me. She never asked me about the button on my shorts, and I was glad because I thought I might get in trouble.

The next time we went to Sheila's house her husband was there. I asked where Brian was and walked to the back of the house.

"Hi, Brian."

"You're just a little baby. Get out of here and leave me alone!" he yelled.

That was the last time I saw him.

*   *   *   *   *

Mr. & Mrs. Dixon lived in a little duplex across the street from us. They invited me over, and while Mrs. Dixon served us cool aid and cookies, Mr. Dixon taught me how to play chess. It only took me a few times to get good at it. I knew that Mr. Dixon let me beat him sometimes, but the more I played, the better I got, and a few times I really did beat him.

In the end apartment of our triplex were a bunch of neighbors. They were nice to me but I could tell they didn't like me around because they stayed up all night long, and I probably woke them up a lot of time with my loud singing, pretending to be Marie Osmond with her bright, shiny teeth, and roller skating up and down the walkway in front of their door. I don't know how many people lived there, because so many were in and out of the place. But I knew George was the main guy. He seemed okay once he got to know me, but I could tell he still didn't like me around much. I guess it made him mad when my friends and I knocked on his door and ran around the building, laughing and hiding. George had long hair and a mustache, and reminded me of my Uncle Charlie, because he was loud and rough. He seemed old to me, but he always had young girls at his place. George didn't live there long because he died in a motorcycle accident. After that, some lady moved in and she never talked to anyone.

In the middle apartment was Marcus. I skated up and down our walkway and saw him go to his car in the blue clothes he wore everyday. He drove a big station wagon with wooden side panels and a Woody Woodpecker sticker on the back window. Woody Woodpecker was one of my favorite cartoons.

"Hi!" I said, "How are you?"

"Hi," he said back. He had big frizzy hair just like my brown teacher at school.

"What's your name?" I asked.

"Marcus," he answered.

"Why do you where the same clothes everyday?" I asked.

"I don't," he said. "I wear them for work."

I knew that he drove a big garbage truck and brought home junk he found that people threw out. For my birthday he gave me a new, giant teddy bear that I combed like a real bear. I ran around calling him "Marcus Parkus" because I couldn't think of anything else that rhymed with his name. He joked around and called me "Susanno". Marcus became friends with Mommy and Daddy and started coming over more often. Sometimes Mommy and I went to his apartment, and they would talk and smoke funny smelling stuff from a big long tube. Marcus's apartment was stinky like smelly cats and smoke, and it wasn't very clean. His clothes were all over the floor, and the bathroom had hair and gross stuff all over it. Marcus didn't lock his apartment when he left, and sometimes I went inside to look around and play with his ugly cat named Bubba and her kittens. One time I went in his apartment to use the bathroom and saw magazines with naked girls in them doing gross things. When I told Mommy, Marcus stopped leaving his door unlocked, and I was told I wasn't allowed over if he wasn't home. I liked Marcus, but sometimes he got on my nerves because he yelled at me for no reason.

"Why do you wear the same clothes everyday?" I asked him again.

"God's hamlet! I don't wear the same plucking clothes everyday! It's a plucking uniform!" he yelled.

"It's a uniform, Susanna," Mommy said sternly. "It looks like the same thing but he wears clean ones everyday."

I figured it had something to do with plucking garbage, so I stopped asking.

* * * * *

I had a lot of friends near my house. Jessica and Sammy lived with their mom a few streets away in an apartment just like ours, but theirs was dirty and had fleas. Mommy said they were nice girls but dirty kids. They said that their mom left their dad a long time ago, because he beat her up. Sammy was Jessica's older sister; she talked a lot and told us jokes with a lot of bad words in them. Their mom had a big book in her bedroom closet all about sex with pictures of naked people that Jessica showed me when we were alone. They didn't have much food at their house, so I hated spending the night because there wasn't anything to eat. When their water got turned off, we scraped ice off of the top of the freezer to drink. If she wasn't at work, Jessica and Sammy said their mom was out drinking. One day they had to move because they couldn't pay rent.

The best friend that I ever had in the neighborhood was Stephanie. She moved to Florida from the snow. We built forts in the woods behind her house and played Barbies all day long when we didn't have school. We had the biggest Barbie collection that was so big, we used our toes to hold dolls up because our hands were full. But Stephanie's brother took care of that for her by destroying them in the woods behind the house.

Stephanie and I loved listening to the radio and singing along to Kenny Rogers. We made up our own songs like, "Marcus Parkus, the garbage man. He plucks the garbage from the garbage can!"

I don't think Marcus liked that very much, because he started being mean and grouchy, so we secretly started calling him Oscar the Grouch.

One day I decided that Marcus made other people mad, too, because I saw Daddy take a broom and smash it in half across the oak tree in our backyard. I don't know why, but Daddy was yelling and cussing at Marcus. Marcus was laughing about it and Mommy was, too. I got scared and started crying. Then Daddy started calling Marcus an egghead all the time.

Chapter Three
The Hartigans

One night Mommy woke me up and told me to get in the car, even though I was still in my pajamas. She was upset, and it seemed like it took a long time to get wherever we were going in her little blue Mustang. When we got to a road with trees hanging over it, Daddy was standing there. I heard Mommy say something to Daddy about Angie, but I don't know who Angie was. I think Daddy was at Angie's house. Mommy yelled at Daddy, and then drove off crying. I started crying, too, because I thought she ran over Daddy's foot. She said she hadn't, and then we drove to Gramma's where I spent the night.

I was in second grade when Mommy sat me down right after Christmas and told me that her and Daddy were getting a divorce, which meant they wouldn't be married and that Daddy wouldn't be living with us anymore. I didn't understand why things were changing so I laid on Mommy's lap and cried while she stroked my face and hair behind my ear until I fell asleep.

Daddy moved into an apartment that was part of a big house in an old neighborhood. I thought his house might be haunted because it seemed old, dark and scary, and it smelled like mold. I visited him every two weekends; during the day I went outside to pick up the nuts that fell off of the tree; at night I watched TV and ate ice cream and slept on the couch. Other times he took me to Grandmaw's when he had dates, but I didn't like staying there because I had to sleep in a room at the end of the long, dark scary hallway, where cousin Wade said the Boogey Man was. Cousin Wade always made me walk down the long hallway with the light on and when I got all the way to the end, he turned off the light and yelled, "The Boogey Man is coming!" I cried every time.

Mommy started going out with Marcus right after the divorce. I got mad at Marcus because he saw Mommy naked in the bathroom, and then he moved in with us. They got into fights a lot and Mommy cried, but Marcus bought her a ring. I guess that made her happy, because they got married after that.

That's when Daddy started taking me every weekend instead of every other weekend. Spending time with him meant doing things that I wasn't able to do at home. Mommy said it was because Daddy had money, and Daddy said it was because Marcus spent his money on booze and cigarettes. Daddy didn't like Marcus very much.

On Fridays Daddy picked me up and took me out for a hamburger meal at my favorite place. If he really felt like splurging, we went to Chuck E. Cheese. Then we'd go to the arcade or the boardwalk or the movies. We still went water skiing with Daddy's boat, sometimes with his girlfriend, and we'd meet friends from the island. I loved going to the island because everyone there had fun; it was nothing like being at home.

Daddy was seeing a woman with red hair and a big chest named Candice. She taught me how to pick honeysuckle flowers, pull them apart, and suck the nectar. Candice had a big pool at her house. She let me swim for as long as I wanted until my fingers and toes were all wrinkled up like raisins. She was Daddy's first girlfriend after the divorce, and even though there were a few others that he dated, Candice was my favorite. I wanted them to get married, but they broke up.

Daddy drove a big black van that we took camping on weekends and up to the mountains when I didn't have school. I thought Daddy's van was cool, because it had ships and skulls on the windows, a bed in the back where I could sleep and play dolls, a wooden barrel chair, and a stereo. I was short enough to stand in front of the front seat and hang onto the dashboard while he drove, and I sang along to all of my favorite songs on the radio by The Lipps and Blondie. I loved spending time with my Daddy.

Daddy worked some weekends in a lab that tested water. When he took me along, we drove out to the middle of nowhere, and he went into the woods to fill up a cup with dirty water. Then we went to his lab where he let me use things called filters and beakers and look into a microscope at creatures living in the water. I felt like I was a real scientist!

Daddy lived in his apartment for a little while before he moved in with Grandmaw and Grandpaw to help them pay bills. I looked forward to spending Saturday with Grandmaw while Daddy worked on the computer or studied for his college classes.

Grandmaw took my cousins and me to the flea market and every weekend to let us sample all of the food so she didn't have to buy us lunch. She sewed and made crafts to sell, and she sewed all three of us granddaughters the same purple outfits that we wore every weekend.

Grandmaw told us the story about her life; her education was only up until the fifth grade because she had to go to work, and she married Grandpaw when she was fifteen years old. She had a big hole in her leg because they removed one of the bones when she was a kid because they were too poor to go to a hospital. Grandmaw said she had only one pair of shoes when she was a kid and they lived in the Carolina's. Her and Grandpaw talked funnier than I did, but when I was around them long enough I started talking like them, too.

Grandpaw never talked much, especially after his throat operation. He got throat cancer from smoking cigarettes without filters, and the doctors had to cut up his larynx. He was grouchy a lot, but maybe it was because we were interrupting him during his western TV shows. Or maybe he was thinking about when he was in the war and his buddy got shot. Grandmaw said it was because Grandpaw wasn't feeling good.

When he was feeling good, Grandpaw took us fishing down at the creek. He made us dig in the dirt for worms, and when I gagged he told me it was because I was a Yankee kid. I knew that had something to do with Mommy, but I didn't know what it meant. He took us for walks in the woods with their dog named Dog. Grandmaw said we could never go alone in the woods because of snakes and bears, and she always yelled at Grandpaw to be careful. Grandpaw always grumbled back at her something about being a grown man and a woman nagging him all of the time.

Daddy was the youngest of the five living kids. His brother - my Uncle Charlie - was the ugliest, meanest, and scariest man I'd ever met. He only had two and a half toes on one foot, because he accidentally shot the others off with a shotgun. He reminded me of the Muppet named Animal because had hair all over his face and body, and he scared little kids. Mommy said that Uncle Charlie had killed animals, and she wouldn't be surprised if he'd ever killed a person and dumped the body in the woods across the street from Grandmaw's house. For a while he was with a really pretty lady who had a boy that I called cousin Billy. Uncle Charlie was crazy, always picking fights with people and yelling and cussing and always calling black people bad names. Sometimes he lived with Grandmaw and Grandpaw when he lost his job. I didn't like going over there. I liked when he got with Aunt Jackie, because that's how I got my cousin Mandy.

Aunt Nadine lived with Grandmaw and Grandpaw sometimes, too. When she was younger she was beautiful and was as sweet as anyone you could ever meet. Mommy said Aunt Nadine could have been a bikini model. I guess something happened to her because she went crazy. Someone said she went to a psychic and never was the same again. I also heard she went crazy after she got beat up by her husband enough times. The worst story that went around about Aunt Nadine was that she was gang raped by a bunch of black men and that she lost a baby that they think was black. I don't know what happened to her one way or another, but I know I didn't like it when she wasn't on her medication. That meant she would get really crazy - like the time we went to the shopping mall, and Aunt Nadine accused people there of stealing the boots out of her closet. Another time she accused Uncle Charlie of stealing her underwear, and Uncle Charlie laughed at her like a hyena, which really set her off. Sometimes she spit at us and started fights and talked to herself while she stomped up and down the hallway back to where the Boogey Man was. I was afraid to sleep in the house with Aunt Nadine there, because I didn't know if she would try to kill me like the time she said she was going to kill Grandmaw and Grandpaw.

Daddy's other sister, Aunt Marylou, was almost as mean as Uncle Charlie sometimes. I didn't know what to think of her, because sometimes she was as unpredictable as Aunt Nadine. When she was nice she had a big smile on her face and laughed, but then she changed in a moment's notice and start yelling at us kids about something that we didn't think we did wrong.

When I was four years old I begged Aunt Marylou to teach me how to ride a bike like cousin Wade because I wanted to be like the big kids. He was her son, older than me by a few years. At first Aunt Marylou said no, because I was a girl and too young to ride a two-wheeled bike, but I begged her. She didn't seem to like it but agreed to let me try.

When I got on the bike, my feet couldn't reach the pedals. Since I had no balance, I fell on the hard pavement. I could hardly stay on the bike, much less pedal it. Aunt Marylou told me to get on the bike, and she helped push me to get me going. I only made it a few feet, lost my balance and fell over. I got up and tried it again. Aunt Marylou helped push me again, but I fell over after a few feet. I guess that made Aunt Marylou mad because she smacked me really hard with her open hand on my back right between my shoulders. She knocked the wind right out of me and made me cry.

I didn't want to ride anymore. The boys laughed at me.

"You better get on that bike or I'm gonna beat your little ass!" she squinted her eyes at me.

I believed her that she would beat me; she was mean like that. I got back on the bike just as she said, even though I didn't want to.

"Don't you fall off," she squinted her eyes at me again. "Or I'm gonna beat your little ass."

I turned to see Wade laughing at me. It kind of hurt my feelings, but I was going to prove to all of them that I could do it. I didn't care that I was only a girl because I saw other girls riding bikes in my neighborhood. Being a girl wasn't going to stop me!

I squeezed the handlebars, barely wrapping my hands around them, and Aunt Marylou gave me a little push to get me going. I pedaled about three feet forward before my balance gave out for the last time. Even though I tried with every last bit of determination in my bones, I couldn't ride that bike. Since I kept falling and scraping up my legs on the road, Aunt Marylou spanked me and told me that I shouldn't be playing with boys and to get in the house and take a nap.

I went inside her dark house and lay in the bed and cried. I listened to the other kids outside having fun. I didn't think it was fair of her to be so mean to me just because I was a girl. I didn't trust her much after that, and after I told Mommy what happened, I didn't have to go over her house by myself again. Even after she put Jesus in her heart and married a preacher, Aunt Marylou still had that mean streak in her eyes.

Mommy said the only normal sister my Daddy had was my Aunt Gena. She had two kids and a Vietnam veteran-turned-biker husband who liked to park his motorcycle in the living room. He scared me, because he had a big white beard, and he never talked to us; he just grumbled. But I got over that when he started playing Santa Claus. Aunt Gena wasn't mean like Aunt Marylou or crazy like Aunt Nadine. She yelled at us sometimes, too, but we usually deserved it. She worked a regular job and never got into fights with the rest of the family like the others did. Maybe that's why she didn't come around Grandmaw's much.

* * * * *

During the summer, Daddy took me to meet my aunts and uncles and cousins in the mountains. I was glad to have someone my own age there. My cousin Shelby and I brought our empty Coke bottles to the tiny store with the old gas pumps. We traded them in for money so we could buy bottles of Yoo-Hoo, and then we went back to my aunt's to swim in the pool.

We visited Silver Dollar City where Daddy flirted with the pretty girls. Grandmaw and Grandpaw came with us, and we dragged Uncle Charlie along. Daddy took a picture of me standing next to one of the girls in a western costume and another one of me sitting in a wheelbarrow with Uncle Charlie holding it up and pushing me along. After Daddy snapped the picture, Uncle Charlie dumped me out of the wheelbarrow onto the gravel. Grandmaw yelled at him, and Daddy called him a bad word.

We visited places where the Cherokee Indians made dolls and carvings and leather shoes. Grandmaw told me we had some Cherokee in us, too. While we rode in the van and Daddy drove, she put my hair in braids and told me how pretty I looked and how much it brought out the Cherokee in me.

"You got cheekbones and skin colored like the Cherokees," she told me. "Look at her, Paw!" She turned to Grandpaw.

"Hey little Injun. You look like a squaw!" Grandpaw said.

I didn't know what he meant by that because I thought engines were for trains and birds squawked, and I didn't think I looked like either a bird or a train. Since he was hard to understand because of his accent and his voice box being cut up, I thought maybe it was some secret Indian language.

"Oh Paw, she looks precious," Grandmaw's raspy voice corrected him. "He don't mean nothin' by it darlin'. An Injun is just an Indian. My momma was half Indian, ya know. We was Cherokee. You see, them white men, they didn't get along with Indians when they was kids. Grandpaw's grandpa came from Ireland and they swam across the ocean to get here. Indians was already here before them, and then they'd have these big wars. Grandpaw was in the war, you know."

"Them Injuns'd scalp them cowboys right up!" Grandpaw said. "They'd cut your hair right off your head like they did to animals."

"Don't scare her paw! You been watchin' too many Westerns," Grandmaw told him.

"She's a Yankee girl anyway, ain't ya?" Grandpaw said to me, leaning in closer and looking at me with his pretty blue-green eyes and shiny white-yellow hair. "You a Yankee like your Yankee grandpaw."

Injuns. Squaws. Yankees. Sometimes I never knew what they were talking about, but I still laughed right along with them.

"She's too young to understand, Paw," Grandmaw said, turning and hugging me. "Grandmaw loves ya, darlin'!"

* * * * *

Grandmaw got Daddy to go to a big church called Calvary where Aunt Marylou went, and he became born again. That meant that he loved Jesus, who was the only person to show him how Daddy was getting to Heaven. They told me I should be born again too, but I decided that I would be baptized with the Holy Spirit. The spirit part scared me, because I thought that God's son was a ghost. One night I was baptized in a big bathtub at the big Calvary church in front of a big audience. That's when they handed me a microphone and I told them I love Jesus, even though I wasn't sure I trusted Him, because I was afraid that I wouldn't go to Heaven with the rest of my family if I didn't do exactly as He said in the Bible. I think that water must have been dirty because I got sick a few days later. Maybe it was because my sins were still washing away.

I wasn't sure I liked the Calvary church because it was boring and they made us read like they did in school instead of color and do crafts like some of the other churches we went to. Besides, they made me feel stupid when I didn't know what some of the Bible meant.

I stopped liking the Sunday school after they asked us what we knew about Abraham. I raised my hand. I knew all about Abraham from school.

"Abraham was the sixteenth president of the United States!" I proudly announced.

"No," the teacher scrunched up his face. "We're talking about Abraham from the Bible."

I guess he thought I was a dumb kid because he never called on me again. I liked the story about the president Abraham better anyway because he freed the slaves.

Grandmaw stopped going to the Calvary church because they asked for too much money. She started going to the new little Pentecostal church next to her house. I wasn't sure I liked that one much either, because the music was old and boring just like most of the people. The congregation was a bunch of people raising their hands and talking in a funny language they said was their tongue. I thought my tongue looked the same as theirs and that they were making it all up, because no one made sense.

The preacher made people go to the stage at the front of the church and yelled at them and pushed them on their head until they fell over onto the floor, raising their hands in the air and crying for Jesus. I hoped they never did that to me because I would probably be asking Jesus for help, too. The first time I saw all of that yelling it made me want to vomit. It scared me to think that God only loved people that talked like they did.

Grandmaw brought my cousin Aurora to church with us sometimes. I was glad I had someone to keep me company while we giggled and mocked them, "La la lah ala blah la blah!"

After we got caught, we had to look at the floor and secretly at each other to make sure Grandmaw didn't see us. The time we did get caught she gave us the look. If we got in trouble with Grandmaw, we all knew what that meant – we'd have to pick out our own hickory stick for a whoopin'.

The only part I liked about going to that church was when Grandmaw gave me mints out of her purse or when they had food after the service because I was always starving by the time it was over. Other than that, I couldn't wait to leave.

Chapter Four
Gramma

After the divorce, Mommy and I still lived in the apartment, and she still brought me to Gramma's in the morning before work. Gramma brought me to school on her moped because she didn't have a driver's license. She said she couldn't drive a car, but one time I saw her back Papa's big boat of a car right into a fence at Aunt Dot's house in Green Cove Springs. She bent a pole right in half.

"Shhh… don't tell Papa," she said, getting out of the car.

"I won't," I giggled.

Gramma and I had our own secrets.

She and Papa bought my brown suede shoes for the school year, and since my birthday was right before school, most of my presents were school clothes and school supplies.

I didn't like second grade as much as first grade. I don't think anyone in my class liked being in second grade. Our teacher, Mrs. Briggs, was a very large dark-brown-skinned lady, like the color of coffee without the milk in it, and she yelled at us kids and told us we were all dumb and stupid.

Mrs. Briggs had a pretty teacher's aide, Ms. Nikita, whose skin was the color of caramel candy. She was in college and helped Mrs. Briggs grade our papers and helped us with our work. Mrs. Briggs was a lot nicer when Ms. Nikita was around.

"How old are you, Ms. Nikita?" I asked her.

"Twenty-one," she replied.

"Why do you work here?"

"I'm going to school to be a teacher," she told me.

"I wish you were our teacher."

She smiled.

"How old is Mrs. Briggs?" I asked.

She glanced over at Mrs. Briggs and whispered under her breath, "About fifty."

I could tell she didn't like our teacher, either. I heard the other teachers whispering about it, and they never sat with our teacher at the field. They sat with Ms. Nikita but never with our teacher. We missed Ms. Nikita when she left because it meant Mrs. Briggs had more time to yell at us, and it meant missing more recess.

I hated math. I didn't understand times tables, and Mrs. Briggs called me stupid. She made us write them over and over until our hands cramped up. Only one girl in the class knew multiplication; she was Mrs. Briggs' favorite, because she didn't have to write them. Instead, she called out times tables out to us as fast as she could every single day after lunch. We hated her because we never got to go to recess. All because she knew times tables and we didn't.

Gramma picked me up everyday after school on her moped and brought me to her house. After a snack, she took me swimming at the pool with all of the other old people. Most of them had known me since I was a baby and every time they saw me they said, "Oh my! You've gotten so big! You're so tall!" Even though I wasn't tall at all compared to kids in my class.

"Your legs are so long! You could be a model," I was often told, even though I didn't know having long legs meant I could be a model.

I liked most of the people there, except for the guy that dunked me. At first it was a fun game until he held me under and I swallowed too much water. Papa yelled at him to stop, that he could hurt me, and that the game was over.

There was always at least one grouchy old lady that yelled at me for splashing whenever I jumped off of the diving board. We nicknamed her Sarge because she bossed everyone around.

"Get away from the pool and go home if you don't want to get wet!" Gramma yelled back.

She got mad and left, mumbling that kids shouldn't be allowed at the pool and were probably peeing in it.

"Those damn old bags shouldn't be up here," Gramma huffed and puffed. "They make me so damn mad. It's a pool for cry sakes. I know they're the ones peeing in the pool because they swim in there for hours without getting out. Bunch of old farts!"

I swam and played in the pool either with anyone who was there or by myself until Gramma told me we had to go home before I get waterlogged. She didn't swim because she didn't know how, but I got her to go in the pool with me once, even though she stayed at the shallow end.

I got to see Nana a lot, too. Gramma and I went to Nana's house for cookies. Most of the time she was sitting in her special rocking chair knitting a blanket or slippers with pom-poms. She always gave me a great big hug, along with a sloppy whiskery kiss on my cheek. Her whiskers felt like a man that forgot to shave.

"Oh daaah-ling!" Nana cried in her Cajun accent.

Sometimes she cried for real because she said she missed us, even though she just saw us the week before. Gramma said she's full of it, that Nana likes people to feel sorry for her and that she was putting on an act.

Nana wore a hearing aid but still couldn't seem to hear anything we said. In order for her to hear us, we had to yell. Most of the time we repeated ourselves at least three or four times, but she still couldn't hear us. Or she thought we said something else. So we gave up and allowed her to make up whatever she thought we said. We all learned it was easier to agree with her, even if it didn't make any sense. Since she couldn't hear well she also yelled when she spoke, with a really high-pitched laugh that pierced our eardrums. Gramma said a few beers always made Nana laugh at everything and her hearing worse.

Like most of the other old people that used to ride around the park, Nana had a giant tricycle. I loved when she let me take it for a ride. It was a safe place for anyone to ride bikes.

"They don't speed down the road around here like those damn kids," Gramma said.

When I was small enough, I sat in the basket on the back of the three-wheeled bike while Nana rode me around.

"Faster! Faster!" I'd yell.

"Hah?" she'd screech.

"Faster!" I yelled, cupping my hands around my mouth to aim the sound towards her.

"Nana's going as fast as she can. Nana's old you know," she said as if she were talking in third person.

I liked visiting Nana, but I didn't like Grampa because he was grouchy and said weird things and repeated himself. Every time I saw him, his funny white fuzzy hair on top of his head looked like he just woke up. He wore plaid shorts and either a white t-shirt or a button up collared shirt if he were going somewhere, and he always had a glass of beer in his hand. I don't think he liked kids much, either, because he yelled at me a lot.

"He's a drunken jerk," Gramma said.

He wasn't her real father. She never knew her real father.

On our way back from Nana's, Gramma took me to visit my Great Aunt Gabby. She owned a neurotic poodle that always jumped up and scratched my legs, barked incessantly, and peed on the floor. She was a very intelligent woman that enjoyed crossword puzzles and playing her piano, but she was always nervous and she seemed to shake a lot. Gramma said Aunt Gabby never left the house after dark because she was afraid of getting raped.

Aunt Gabby seemed very tall compared to Gramma, and she always wore white flat old lady shoes and flowery dresses that looked like nightgowns. I thought she might be pregnant because her belly stuck out even though she was skinny everywhere else.

"Is Aunt Gabby going to have a baby?" I asked Gramma.

Gramma laughed, "Noooo…."

"Why does her belly stick out like that?"

"That's what happens when you get old."

I overheard that one time Aunt Gabby had a baby and lost it, and I figured maybe that was why her belly still stuck out. It was lost somewhere in her belly.

Since Gramma didn't drive, Aunt Gabby took us shopping on longer trips. I hated it because I sat in the backseat of her big silver Buick, almost throwing up every time. She sped up and then hit her brakes every few seconds. Gramma made me drink ginger ale to soothe my belly. She always knew how to make me feel better.

* * * * *

I miss being able to visit Gramma as much as I used to since the move, because now we live too far for me to ride a bike.

I like spending weekends with her and getting to see Nana again.

"Stop pickin'," Gramma gripes, lightly slapping my hand away from my arm.

I have been picking my arms since fourth grade. I don't know why I do it, but if I see one flaw, I want it gone. By the end of my picking sessions, both of my entire upper arms are red with bumps, scarred from my fingernails. I squeeze anything I can that doesn't look normal to me.

"Why do you do that?" Gramma asks. "You're going to scar your arms and you won't be able to wear pretty things when you're older."

"I have pimples."

"You're going to have scars on your arms, and that's going to look worse than pimples. Believe me. Just don't do it."

"I can't help it," I tell her.

Sometimes I hide so that I can pick my arms without getting yelled at. Most of the time my shirtsleeves cover them, and within a few days everything is healed. As soon as I see another bump, I am at it again.

"I've never seen anyone pick, pick, pick like you do. It's not good. You're going to ruin your arms."

I'm not concerned with ruining my arms as much as I am concerned with making the things go away. It is one of the only things that Gramma can't seem to fix.

Chapter Five
Bianca

The Pentecostal church is where Daddy met Bianca, and four months later they are married. I like her. Daddy is happy. She tries teaching me how to do girly things - like bake cakes and wear frilly dresses and all of the things that Mom doesn't do. Bianca makes me eat gross things like Brussels sprouts and spaghetti sauce with carrots. I figure it's because she is from Canada, and Grandmaw says that Canadians are weird.

Daddy moves into a nice house with Bianca, and when he tells me he needs to spend more time with his new wife and less with me on the weekends, my stomach hurts. That means I am stuck at home with Marcus.
"That fake blonde witch doesn't want you around," Mom snarls. "She wants all of your father's attention."

Mom hates Bianca. She always has an irritated look on her face whenever I talk about her, especially when I tell Mom about all of the things Bianca and I do together. Mom says she doesn't want to hear about it anymore, so I never talk about our fun times again. I think Mom is jealous because she always talks about Bianca's blonde hair and big chest that hangs out everywhere.

With a tap dance recital coming up, I send out invitations to the whole family, just like I did last year. Bianca tells me that she and Daddy won't be there, because dance recitals are all vanity. I am upset that Daddy can't tell me himself, because he went the year before with Grandmaw and had no problems with it. Mom is upset, too.

"Who is she kidding? That bitch that wears more makeup than the girls in the show! She's just jealous because she has a big fat ass and doesn't want your father looking at prettier, skinnier girls on stage!"

There are some things that I don't like about Bianca. She makes me go to church when I don't want to go; she makes me raise my hands to praise the Lord even though it makes me feel embarrassed; and she makes me wear her old clothes, even though they are two to three sizes too big for me and made for a grown woman. She says they look fine on me, but the kids at school laugh and ask me what the heck am I wearing.

Then Bianca cut my hair.

Bianca has a way of making everyone believe her. She says she always cuts Daddy's hair and her own, so I agree to let her cut mine after church. I look in the mirror a few times while she works on it, but I don't like what I see. I think maybe she can fix it and allow her to keep cutting. But when I look in the mirror for the last time, I see that my beautiful, healthy, long dark hair has gone from being about eight inches below my shoulders to a shaggy, cropped mullet. I start crying, put on a painter's hat, and run out the front door. At first I don't know where I am going. Since it is only about two miles up the road, I decide to walk to Grandmaw's.

The first person I see is Aunt Jackie.

"Oh hi, Susanna," Aunt Jackie says. "I didn't know that was you. I thought it was a boy walking down the road."

I cry harder. I know Aunt Jackie doesn't mean to hurt my feelings, but what she said is true. I do look like a boy. She hugs me, goes inside and tells Grandmaw about it.

"Why did she do that to your pretty hair, honey?" Grandmaw seems sad.

"She said she could cut it like I wanted it," I tell her.

Uncle Charlie is shaking his head.

"That old bar whore can't cut hair! She ain't never went to school for that," he speaks very loudly.

Grandmaw calls Daddy to come get me. Bianca gives him my things and makes Daddy drive me home alone.

"Your hair doesn't look that bad," he tells me.

I keep quiet the whole ride home. Mom is standing outside when we pull up to the house. I say goodbye to Daddy and he leaves.

"What did you do to your hair?" she looks horrified.

"Bianca cut it."

"I don't like it," she frowns. "She should have left your hair alone. Why did you let her do it?"

"I don't know," I cry. "She told me she could cut hair. I thought she knew what she was doing."

"She cuts your father's hair and look at his!" She is mad. "She doesn't know what she's doing! That bitch!"

Mom stomps off to call Bianca and give her a piece of her mind, which usually means saying a few four letter words and mentioning Jesus Christ or God's hamlet, even though I don't think they have anything to do with it.

I want to go to school tomorrow, except that I don't want anyone to see my hair. I pick at my arms, pondering what to do about it and decide that putting it up in pigtails will be the easiest way to hide the awful cut.

*   *   *   *   *

I like Mrs. Esser. She is my favorite teacher and also my new teacher, because moving to the new house meant I almost had to change schools. I am in the middle of sixth grade and begged to stay at my school. The school people said the only way I could stay was for me to be put in the gifted program. I took a bunch of tests and passed. I hated having to leave my friends to be with the smart kids from down the hall, but at least I am still able to see them. I didn't know that I am as smart as the gifted kids.

Mrs. Esser talks to me like I am a real person. She is different from all the other teachers I've had. She is smart and takes us on fun field trips and brings us neat things from the radio station, like hats and spring break t-shirts with beer advertisements on them. Everyone loves her.

Mrs. Esser knows that it's difficult for me to be the new girl in her class. Except for a few of the boys and a few quiet girls that never talk to anyone, the others in class pick on me. I think she tries to keep the others away from me as much as possible so I can concentrate more on my schoolwork than having to worry about being made fun of by the rich kids. All of those kids live in nice houses. I would *die* if they ever saw mine.

Mrs. Esser asks me what happened to my pretty hair. I tell her, and she agrees that it's a chopped up mess. She talks to Mom and takes me to get a real haircut and ice cream. I didn't know that teachers cared about kids after school.

When Mrs. Esser drops me off at home after my haircut I am embarrassed that she sees our yucky old house. I think she knows that I hate going home after school, too. I don't know how much Mrs. Esser actually knows about me, but that woman is smart and no one can pull the wool over her eyes.

I wonder how much she really knows.

Chapter Six
Holidays

The longer the holiday vacation, the more I dread it. For at least two weeks each December, a half of a week in November, plus a week during the spring, while everyone else looks forward to going on vacations, hanging out with friends, and having fun, I feel as if I am the only kid in the world wishing that I am still in school.

Before Marcus came along, I enjoyed the holidays. But with him around, there is sure to be an argument or other miserable time, listening to him complain and snark about everything, especially anything I do. It also means he drinks more. There are no parties, no friends, and no true laughter except to ridicule others. The only family gatherings I look forward to are at Gramma and Papa's because it is the only time that I feel safe from Marcus's barking at my every little move.

Other family gatherings involve being with Marcus's weird family. His father (whom Mom secretly calls Hitler because he is a tyrant and has a dark mustache) refers to all children as "rotten little kids". I am no exception, but the name-calling doesn't end there. Marcus's obedient mother, Rose, is nice most of the time and tries to keep the kids as far from her husband as possible – and he sees to it she does just that.

Just because it's a holiday doesn't exempt them from being freaks. Marcus still refers to me as "The Monster," particularly in front of his own family members, as if to impress them. They laugh and joke about calling me names; even when the babies were born everyone laughed and said they looked like aliens. I guess they think it's okay and normal to make fun of people, especially small children. Sometimes Mom secretly looks at me and rolls her eyes, because she knows they are stupid and immature. Mom never really says anything, though. I think she's afraid, so she pretends to laugh along with them. Rose does the same. I hate being around them.

Hitler has never been nice – never one kind word or gesture - nor does he ever speak to me except to bark out a command or an insult. Because he wears dark eyeglasses that hide his eyes, no one knows what he is looking at. Hitler served time in a Florida prison for embezzling money when he worked for the city. On top of that, he is weird and creepy and always stinks because he doesn't wear deodorant. He isn't very nice to the babies, either. When we moved out of their trailer and into the new ugly house, Mom discovered a peephole in the bedroom wall. Hitler had been secretly watching her.

Marcus's younger brother, Melvin, is the only one in their family who is remotely nice to me. He flirts with me, and everyone else seems to think it's cute and funny – even though I am only in sixth grade. I think it's weird. Melvin is married to a teenaged girl from his high school. They're going to have a baby together. Melvin also went to jail for tying up and having sex with a girl the same age as me.

Marcus's older brother, Arthur, is just as weird as the rest of them. Most of the time he keeps quiet, but when he speaks he says stupid things. And he smells like a troll. Every time Arthur holds the babies under his arms, Mom has to wash their heads because their uncle does not wear deodorant. No wonder he never has a girlfriend.

* * * * *

On the first Christmas while we lived with Rose and Hitler, as I opened gifts, I thought I saw another gift. It turned out to be wrapping paper sitting in a shape of a box.

Being that I always ask permission before reaching for anything, I asked, "Is that it?"

Had I known that those three words would cause such a scene, I'd have never said them.

What I meant was "Is that another box?" but it was misconstrued as "Is that all?" and I got hell for it.

"What? Is that *it*?" Rose said, as if I had committed a crime. "What do you mean *is that it*?"

Her crying out attracted the attention of everyone else.

"What do you mean *is that it*?" Marcus repeated. "You mean this wasn't enough for you?"

"I didn't mean it like that," I tried defending myself, feeling both ashamed and embarrassed. My stomach knotted up, my throat tightened. "I thought there was something in a box."

"What a brat!" Rose stated in a high-pitched voice, as if she had been taken by surprise. "Like you didn't get enough! I should take this stuff back."

"That's not what I meant," I tried defending myself again.

But no one listened. No one cared. Defending myself was virtually impossible around any of those people. And I didn't care if she took her stupid stuff back. I wished she hadn't even given me anything. It was mostly dumb old school supplies anyway. It wasn't worth being made to feel this bad on Christmas.

"What a selfish brat!" Marcus continued. "You should be happy you got anything at all! You got more than any of us ever got…"

Marcus continued to repeat himself about what a selfish brat I was. I felt like a horrible person. It would be the first of many ruined holidays since Mom married Marcus. Nothing was fun anymore.

* * * * *

Sometimes holidays seem like they are going fine until Marcus says something to destroy the joy.

"Are you going to see your dad today?" Rose asks.

"Yes, I'm going to see Daddy and my other grandma later," I tell her.

"Daddeeee," Marcus mocks me in a snobbish, nasally tone, while he and his stupid stinky father and brothers laugh, as if I can't hear them.

"Daddy buys her whatever she wants," Marcus tells everyone.

That isn't true at all. The truth is that Daddy buys me things for Christmas or my birthday that I need, like new shoes for church or a bicycle to ride to school. Just because he gives me nice things from the store instead of from the garbage doesn't mean I'm spoiled. Marcus mocks me and says mean things about my Daddy because he knows it makes me furious. He does it at home when no one else is listening. He enjoys taunting me because I am his only witness, and he gets away with it because no one does anything about it. If I get mad or react, he calls me a brat and finds a way to punish me. I know he does it on purpose, but there is nothing I can do about it. He is sneaky.

* * * * *

Holidays with Daddy are much different. At least I don't get yelled at or called names, except maybe by Uncle Charlie. But he doesn't count. Everyone says he's ignorant.

"How's your momma?" Uncle Charlie asks me. "She's fine."

"She still married to that half-breed?" he laughs at his own joke. "She's a pretty woman. What's your momma doin' with a nigger?"

Even though I don't like Marcus, I don't want my mother to be associated with that word.

"Now, Charlie, don't you talk to that child about her momma that way," Grandmaw defends.

Every holiday the entire family goes to Grandmaw's for a big meal, opens presents, and then us kids play outside. Grandmaw gives me homemade gifts she sews. I get a new dress or a doll from my aunts.

But after Daddy married Bianca, things changed and we don't go to Grandmaw's as much.

Chapter Seven
Dread

    The worst time to go home is right after having a good day or a good time. Marcus makes a point to see that my mood goes from sixty to zero in two seconds flat. He spends more energy on making my life hell than he does paying attention to his own kids. As soon as I walk through the door he either yells at me to start doing chores, or he tells me to go straight to my room. There doesn't have to be a reason for it; it's just the way he is. And I have to accept it.

    Sometimes I forget to do a chore, like taking out the garbage, and he punishes me for weeks. The punishments range from doing extra gross chores, like washing out the maggot-filled dumpster by hand (without gloves), to having to go to bed at seven o'clock in the evening for two weeks, even before the babies go to bed. That's how I end up spending so much time in my room reading at my window.

    I also bury myself into my schoolwork so I can make good grades. I enjoy doing homework because it keeps my mind focused on something besides living with a crazy person. Even so, Marcus easily manages to find ways to interrupt my learning experience because he knows how much it bothers me.

    Upstairs in my room with the door closed, enjoying learning and doing homework, I hear the creaking of that third to the last step. I can always tell the difference between his steps and Mom's. His reminds me of a big, heavy ogre's.

This time it isn't Mom's footsteps. My stomach sinks. With my door right in front of the top step, Marcus walks by, cackles his evil laugh, and chortles just loud enough for me to hear.

"You little witch!"

He does things like that all the time without Mom knowing, and I have stopped telling her because it doesn't help.

"Just ignore him," she says.

I ignore the big ogre the best I can, thinking about what a jerk he is and wishing he'd fall down the steps and die.

He opens my door so fast it scares me.

"What are you doing?" he asks.

I am always jumping; he is always trying to catch me in the act of doing something wrong.

"Homework," I reply, matter-of-factly, trying to show him that I have some control over my own life, even though my throat tightens and my heart races.

"Well, you need to get your chores done first! Then you can do homework!" he snaps.

I start complaining to Mom that he shouldn't be walking in on me with the door shut because I might be undressed. He obliges, but then he stands at my door and either does his cackling laugh or yells and knocks loud enough to scare me instead. The knot in my stomach never goes away. Just to ease the tension, I sit in my room and pick when I have no homework.

"You'll never amount to anything," Marcus tells me.

Screw you! I'm going to become something just to spite you.

"Just because you have little tits and a little ass now, you think you're hot shit. You'll be pregnant by the time you're sixteen."

I feel even more disgust towards him. He has no business even thinking about my body, much less say *that* to me. And why does he always tell me I'll wind up pregnant?

Sometimes I finish my chores early. He finds more stupid things for me to do, like sweep the sidewalk – even if it doesn't really need it. Since we have a huge oak tree in front of the house, the leaves are never ending. There are always at least a few leaves, but he thinks that they need to be removed. Every time I finish sweeping, Marcus goes outside and finds another leaf or two that I miss, and then tells me do it all over again. I wonder if he is putting the leaves there himself, since he likes to play those games.

*   *   *   *   *

When we lived at the trailer with his creepy family, Marcus made me sweep the patios and driveways, and he wanted it done before he came home from work. On school days I had to get right to it so he wouldn't yell at me when he got home. I finished about an hour before he got off of work, but by the time he came home, he counted three leaves on the walkway and made me do the entire thing all over again. I knew he watched me out of the window to make sure I didn't screw up.

Everything was a game to him. I started waking up at 6 a.m. to complete my chores so that I could have the rest of the day to ride my bike and play with my friends, like any fourth grader during summer vacation. I wished that Marcus would commend me for getting up so early and doing my work. We had trees everywhere, so by the time Marcus came home I had to redo the entire job because he counted fifteen leaves on the two driveways we shared with his flaky family. It didn't matter that I made a bigger effort than he'd asked. Nothing was ever good enough.

I was nine years old the first time I mouthed off to Marcus. To prove that I knew he was bigger and badder than me, he intimidated and bullied me by pushing his chest out like a chicken and yelling.

"You think you're so tough, don't you," he came at me. "Come on, hit me! Hit me if you think you're so tough!"

So I did. I slapped him as hard as I could with my open hand over and over, yelling at him to stay away from me. His taunts were unrelenting, and no one did anything to stop him. I felt so helpless; I wanted to die.

He finally stopped making me sweep so much in the heat after the day I had a two-hour nosebleed and almost had to go to the hospital. But even then he complained about it.

* * * * *

Marcus makes up lies about everything. At first Mom doesn't believe him, but he has a way of manipulating and convincing her that the sky is green, even though it's blue. If she doesn't believe him, they fight all night. It is a never-ending battle with him.

"See? See? That kid is making us fight again!" he tells her.

When I was eight years old, Marcus accused me of calling him a son of a bitch, which was a lie. He claimed he'd heard me say it when he was in his garbage truck one day when I was on my way to school with Rebekah. Passing him on our bikes and waving, we yelled, "Hi Marcus!"

But he ignored us. Instead, when I got home from school he claimed that one of the guys on the truck heard me call him a son of a bitch. No matter how much I swore that I never said that, and his story changed from one of the guys hearing it to hearing it himself, I was still in trouble. It didn't matter what the truth was.

The truth was this: I hadn't called him a son of a bitch at all; I actually called him an asshole, and it was under my breath so that no one could hear me. But I wasn't about to tell him that.

* * * * *

I walk in from school and go to my room. I notice something on my bed – on my pillow. A gift? I am excited until I realize what it is.

"What is that on my pillow!?" I storm out of my room, down the steps.

I look at Mom.

"What's on your pillow?" She is clueless.

"There's a maxi pad on my pillow!" I yell.

Mom thinks it's a joke, looks at Marcus.

"Did you put a pad on her pillow, Marcus?" Mom asks, puzzled.

"You left it on the bathroom floor. I stepped on it and blood came gushing out," he lies. "I almost got sick."

"You're a liar!" I scream. "A big, disgusting liar! I hate you!"

I storm back to my room. He is the biggest liar I've ever known. There is no blood on it at all, but it doesn't matter what the truth is even if the evidence is in plain view. I don't think Mom believes him, either, because she knows I am not on my period. But instead of speaking up to him, she tells me not to worry about it.

* * * * *

At the old place we didn't have a dining area. While I sat at a stool at the twelve-inch kitchen counter by myself, Mom and Marcus sat in front of the TV in the tiny living area off of Marcus's parent's trailer, eating off of trays. After dinner, my chores were to wash the dishes, dry them, and put them away. I had to lug the tub of dishes into the main part of the trailer to wash them. I'd been doing it since I was eight or nine so it was normal to me, even though I didn't particularly like it. Marcus expected me to have everything perfect, with no spots or food on the dishes, pots and pans, or silverware whatsoever. I thought I did a pretty good job for a kid, but sometimes I missed a spot or two, and Marcus made me re-wash everything, sometimes standing over me, yelling at me to scrub the cheap, crappy, aluminum pots that everything stuck and burned onto, even if it took me all night. I didn't understand why it was okay for him and Mom to let pots soak in water overnight when I wasn't at home, but it wasn't okay for me. I wasn't allowed to spill any water on the counter or the floor, and the dishrag had to be placed a special way on the sink when I finished. If I did one thing incorrectly, there would be hell to pay. There were times I washed dishes for two hours at least - and I cried because I couldn't understand why things were the way they were. It wasn't like I was doing anything on purpose. There was no room for mistakes.

* * * * *

Since dinnertime is dreadful, I hate evenings. Even when I am starving, I prefer eating by myself. I hate looking at him and watching him sit with his head tilted down towards the plate and scraping the food from his fork into his mouth without ever looking up. I try to speak and make normal conversation;

he makes a point to say something to upset my stomach or tells me to shut up and eat. He finishes his food, gets up without excusing or cleaning up after himself, trots into the living room, lights a smelly cigarette, watches TV, and drinks beer. I guess he thinks it was a woman's job to keep quiet and clean up after him.

Chapter Eight
Another Move

I don't want to be here anymore, and this time I'm going to do something about it.

I know we have vitamins in the kitchen. I tiptoe downstairs to get glass of water. While Mom is in the other room, I count out thirty-two little round orange vitamins and swallow them all. I figure they are the safest and most painless pills for me to take if I am going to die. I quietly walk back upstairs to my room, hoping that my plan will work. I lay on my bed, waiting.

About forty-five minutes later, Mom calls me downstairs for something. I feel awful and don't want to go downstairs or see Mom. As soon as I walk into the dining room, I grab a paper plate off the dining table and hurl a thick, green substance onto it, tasting that awful vitamin flavor all over again. As sick as I feel, I am very conscious not to throw up on the carpet or anything that might get me into trouble.

"What's wrong with you?" Mom scowls.

"I don't know," I lie.

She sends me to my room to lie down. I feel awful for the rest of the day, as if I don't feel awful enough, and I learn quickly that a handful of vitamins aren't going to kill me. Another disappointment.

* * * * *

I forgot about the vitamin incident until today. While I was at school, Mom read my diary.

"What did you think you were trying to do?" Mom yells. "Your life isn't that bad!"

It isn't that good either.

I should have known better than to write anything down on paper that I do or feel, because she'd broken into and read my very first diary when I was nine years old – broke the lock right off of it so that she could read it. That time I got in trouble for writing three week's worth of "I hate Marcus" on every page. But it was true. I did hate him. Why couldn't I write how I felt in my own private diary? Marcus took my garbage-found radio and made me stay in my box-sized room for a week. I felt betrayed that Mom told Marcus what I had written.

This time was different. I am older now. I am almost a teenager. I have my periods now, which means that I'm almost a woman and need my privacy. I feel that I deserve some type of respect, but I am told that children have to earn respect. And it certainly isn't given in return. I guess that means children aren't supposed to have feelings, either. They are to be unheard at all times. Even in their own diaries.

* * * * *

Most of my friends think that my parents are strange.

"No one our age goes to bed at 7 o'clock! That's crazy!" they tell me. "And no one has to do those stupid chores twice!"

No one understands why friends aren't allowed over, and neither do I. After the one or two times Allison did come over to spend the night she never came back because Marcus was rude.

He is ignorant towards all of my friends, even if they are well mannered. We aren't allowed to watch TV or do anything; we have to sit in my room and stay quiet, and usually end up watching Scaggly out of my window.

"Sorry Susanna, no offense to you, but your house sucks," Allison says.

Of course I agree, because it is true. Our house does suck. Who can blame her? I don't want to be here, either.

I don't get to go skating with my friends on weekends like I used to because there is never enough gas in the car, and most of the time I'm not allowed to spend the night at my friend's houses. It isn't because I do anything wrong; it's because Marcus has his reasons – like I have to get up with the babies first thing in the morning on the weekends and help Mom. I don't mind babysitting, but taking care of twin babies is quite a chore for a sixth-grade kid. They have to be bathed and fed, burped and changed, and given constant attention. Half of the time the babies wake up early, take off their diapers and smear poop on the walls. Marcus gets to sleep in while Mom and I do all the work. It is expected of me, and I should be thankful for anything that Marcus gives me, according to him, like a roof over my head and the food in the refrigerator – as if I don't deserve to be fed or have a home.

"You think your dad's measly hundred dollars a month pays for you? That hardly pays for the food you eat," Marcus reminds me whenever I need anything.

I stand there, saying nothing, looking at him and think what a ball and chain I must be.

"Your father's money doesn't pay for the roof over your head. I do that," he continues, poking himself in the chest with his index finger, hard enough to hear the thump.

Still standing there and listening to his speech that I've heard a zillion times, I want to kick him in the teeth just once. Just once! I am sick of hearing him repeat himself and reminding me what a nuisance I am to him and my mother.

"I do that," he repeats. "Your dad's money doesn't pay for anything."

The repeating is pure torture. I'd rather spend time in my room with my books or writing or picking.

There is never enough money for food for an entire seven days, but there is always enough money for beer, cigarettes, and pot. Beer and cigarettes come out of the grocery money for the week, no matter what. Gramma and Papa help buy the baby diapers if they run out. They have no idea of the truth, because Mom hides it so well. Considering Marcus drinks at least a six pack a day and smokes a pack of cigs a day, I figure that is about a fifth of where the grocery money goes. That doesn't even include weekends when there is usually some type of football game or race on TV. I dread weekends.

Marcus has a little silver tray where he keeps his rolling papers and bag of weed, and he painstakingly separates the seeds before rolling a joint. I've been watching him do this since my mom and dad were married - when Marcus lived in his smelly apartment next door to us, so I don't know who they think they are fooling. I also have the knowledge that a bag of weed cost at least twenty to twenty-five dollars. I know its peculiar odor, and no matter how many times they try to convince and tell me it is incense, I know better, but I also know to play stupid and pretend it is incense so I don't get yelled at and sent to my room.

Susanna is the one with the wild imagination; Susanna must smell incense every day and doesn't know the difference. Right.

Shopping is done on Friday, and by Wednesday there are usually a couple slices of bread and a cup of milk, maybe a bowl of cereal, peanut butter and jelly, and sometimes Marcus's snacks. I have to ration out milk for the week and enough to make a sandwich to take to school or risk getting yelled at if we run out. When I have growth spurts and eat more than usual, I get yelled at for "eating everything". I can't eat as much as my stomach wants. Marcus buys snacks for himself, like Oreo cookies and rocky road ice cream, but I am forbidden from them. If I take even one Oreo he knows because he counts them or puts them in a certain order just to see if I dare disobey him.

I start buying my own snacks for the week with the money I have saved, but when Marcus finds out I am hiding them in my room, he makes me put them in the kitchen so he can have them, too, and tells me that having snacks in my room is the reason we have roaches. Marcus purposely takes my snacks out and eats them in front of me, knowing how angry it makes me. He makes comments about how good they are, and when he is done, he tells me that I am a selfish brat for not offering him any.

* * * * *

Even though the visits become less frequent, I look forward to visiting Daddy, and I have already forgiven Bianca for butchering my hair. Their house is always warm and cozy. Bianca has down comforters and nice pillows and warm beds, and they have a warm fireplace for the winter, air conditioning for the hot months, and things that I'm not used to having. I am even allowed to take hot baths and sit in the tub for as long as I want!

I have wanted to shave my legs since fifth grade, because my friends are already shaving and making fun of me. Mom says I have to wait until I'm thirteen, but when I speak to Bianca about it, she gives me a razor and tells me to go at it. It must have taken me an hour or more, and I cut myself a few times, but

I am grateful to be able to do at least one thing all of my friends are doing. Plus, I don't have boy legs anymore.

By the middle of the summer between sixth and seventh grades, I decide that I want to live with Daddy and Bianca. They convince me that living with them will be better than living with Marcus and his drinking and drug habits.

I agree, but know that I will miss Mom. I hate the thought of leaving the babies and her alone with Marcus. What if something happens and she needs me? I hesitate calling Mom on the phone because I fear her reaction.

"I don't want to tell her," I say to Dad and Bianca.

"You're the one that has to tell her, not us," Bianca says.

I pick up the phone. Mom answers. I'm crying.

"What's wrong?" she asks.

"I don't want to come home," I say. "I want to stay here."

I can tell she isn't happy. But I also know that I might be in trouble if I do decide to go back home.

"Why don't you come home and we'll talk about it?" she says, but I feel that it is more than a suggestion.

My stomach knots. I can barely swallow. My heart races. I am scared to death and know I cannot turn back now. I cry harder. Daddy takes the phone from me. Bianca hugs me and says everything is going to be all right.

All I have to do is go back there to pack.

Chapter Nine
Four Squares

Moving into a new home doesn't seem that awkward to me. Perhaps it's because I've been wanting this change so badly. I am excited about living in a nice neighborhood and having the luxuries of air conditioning and heating. It also means that I will be attending a new junior high school where most of my friends go. I don't get yelled at all the time, and I don't have to stay in my room all the time.

Since I haven't met too many friends in my new neighborhood, and I am used to spending a lot of time by myself, I've been writing puppet shows for the small children at church. I also write long letters to my cousin Tracy in New England, and I have pen pals in all over the United States.

I turn twelve. Bianca throws me the first real birthday party I've had in a long time. I invite Allison, Brandy, and Fran from my old sixth grade class, and Brandon from church. Bianca makes food and a nice cake, and puts games together for us. It is a great time, but it is our last great time all together.

Our church is called The Four Squares. It's a small Pentecostal church, the same one where Daddy met Bianca. I think Four Squares is a dumb name for a church, but I figure it has something to do with the family of four that runs it. I have to attend church every Sunday morning, Sunday night, and Wednesday night.

Shelly, a large tall girl who wears braces on her teeth, is the pastor's daughter. She's not much fun to be around, because she is way too serious about her Bible. Everything she does must revolve around Jesus, which is a little crazy and boring for me. Since our youth group is mostly boys, Brandon and Justin are my friends. They're more fun to be around anyway, because we like to joke around, not just read the boring Bible and sing hallelujah.

Gertrude, Bianca's mother, goes to our church. I have to spend a few days with her while Daddy and Bianca spend some time together alone. Gertrude is an overweight lady with pretty skin, and she constantly preaches about the Lord. She yells and cries for no reason, calling for Jesus and praying to him to save her marriage from her unfaithful husband. Her yelling and screaming scares me at times, especially when she tells me that the devil is inside of me. That's only if I say or do something she doesn't like. More than anything, that makes me mad, and I feel like telling her the devil must be in *her* since she yells and scares kids away.

There are no kids my age where Gertrude lives except for a poor abused girl across the street. Brittany goes to my school and has a really good heart, but she's an outcast. I feel sorry for her. Her stepmother hates her, she wears the same dirty clothes every day, and the kids in school are really cruel to her – especially the time when Brittany sat on the ground in a short jean skirt with her knees up to her chin, without wearing any underwear. Everyone says she's been sexually abused. Gertrude makes it her mission to get Brittany saved. There is no doubt in Gertrude's mind that this twelve-year-old girl is going to hell unless Jesus intervenes. Brittany goes to church with us a few times, but then her stepmother forbids her from being around Gertrude altogether.

Even though I don't like it, I call Gertrude "Grandma" just to make her happy, and because Bianca makes me. I don't think she deserves it, because my real grandmas have been around my whole life, and this woman is a fruitcake.

Like Bianca, Gertrude has her quirky ways. I don't like any of the food that she cooks. She makes me sit at the table until I finish my food, even though I am determined not to eat it - no matter what she does. I am stubborn like that, so she finally gives up. I don't care that I go to bed hungry, because no food is still better than her yucky Canadian vegetables.

Although she has a two-bedroom mobile home, Gertrude makes me share the bed with her when I stay over. She also makes me listen to awful church music on the radio so she can fall asleep, and then she snores as loud as a pig all night long while I lie awake trying to snuff out the noise with a pillow over my head. I have never heard such an unnatural disturbance in my entire life.

Hearing Gertrude yelling about things isn't unusual, so I don't pay much attention when I hear her squealing in the bathroom. When she comes storming out of the bathroom I don't know what to expect to come out of her mouth next.

"How much toilet paper are you using?!" she shrieks.

Unsure of how to answer such an awkward question, I have to think for a second. I shrug my shoulders. She makes it seem like I have done something really, really bad. Did I clog up the toilet?

"How many squares are you using?" she demands.

Squares?

I almost laugh out loud because I have never heard of anyone counting the squares of toilet paper they use. But I hold my composure. God forbid if I ever laugh at this brute of a woman she'll accuse the devil of being in me, and my head will be doused in holy water.

"I don't know," I answer truthfully. "I just take a handful."

"A handful? You take a handful for your little ass? You only need two squares!"

Her short blonde curly hair bounces from side to side as she shakes her head at me. I look at her, puzzled, thinking she is surely nuts.

"Then I'd get it on my hand," I tell her, wrinkling my nose at the thought of how gross that would be.

"You only need two squares if you pee, and maybe you can have three or four if you're taking a crap. I'll count them for you next time."

Count my toilet paper squares? She is surely joking. I bet Jesus doesn't make anyone count their toilet paper squares.

I chalk it up to her being a cheap Canadian, just like Grandmaw says. I am determined never to stay at her house ever again.

* * * * *

Music is a big part of my life and always has been. It helps me remember things, and I can tell anyone what year a song came out by remembering the age or grade I was in when I first heard it. I have a little radio that I listen to in my room, usually tuned to top 40 music. I like reading teen magazines with all of the latest, greatest posters of pop stars and teen idols, and at the same time I listen to music. I'm not allowed to hang posters in my room because it will ruin the walls, so I keep them in a drawer.

"What are you listening to?" Bianca asks while I am in my room, reading and listening to music. I can see in her face that she doesn't like it, and something is wrong. I am afraid of what I have done.

"Men At Work," I answer timidly.

"I've never heard of them," she says.

I show her a poster of the group from one of my magazines.

"See? Here they are. They have good songs."

"They look gay," she says, crinkling her face.

"Huh? How can you tell?"

I'm not quite sure I understand what gay is, but I know the kids at schools say it means a man liking another man.

"They're gay," she repeats. "You can see it in their eyes. And look at their earrings. It means that they're gay. It's disgusting. Turn this music off, it's making me sick to my stomach."

I am confused. A lot of guys at school wear earrings, but they're not gay; they have girlfriends. And how can a song about Australia make someone ill? I am offended and insulted! After all, something that I enjoy that is perfectly harmless is being used against me.

"But they're not saying anything bad!" I cry.

"I don't care what it's about," Bianca's face contorts. "They're homosexuals and it's satanic! Just turn it off!"

I sulk the rest of the afternoon alone in my room. It's not fair that I have to turn off something I like just because she thinks someone is gay. Who cares if they are gay if the music is good?

* * * * *

I try to keep my radio as quiet as possible and my bedroom door shut now so the music doesn't make Bianca sick.

She opens my door. I am picking my arms.

"What are you doing?" she asks.

I look at her.

"Don't pick at your arms. You're going to scar yourself," she says. "Who is that on the radio?"

"Michael Jackson."

"I don't think it's a good idea to listen to that garbage. The Jacksons are sinners."

She hands me some tapes.

"Here's Amy Grant and Sandi Patty for you to listen to. You like them, right?"

I don't really care for the lame Christian music, but it's better than listening to some of the other awful boring church stuff she has. She shuts the door and I go back to picking, mostly out of boredom.

* * * * *

School starts, and I am both excited and nervous. I have heard all kinds of stories about the new school – mostly good stuff. But during the first two weeks of school, I get lost three times. I don't understand why building 15 is next to building 9, and building 14 is on the other side of campus. What brainiac put this together? The only good part is that we have air conditioning in the ninety-five degree heat.

None of my friends are in any of my classes, and two out of seven teachers are worth liking. The rest of them yell at us.

My bus stop is a few blocks from our house, where I meet Sabrina, an eighth grader. Every day we sit together on the bus and talk about our problems at home. She isn't allowed to play after school or go anywhere because she has to babysit her little brother, and she is never allowed to have anyone over.

"My father is a jerk, and I hate his wife," Sabrina tells me. "She never lets me do anything."

Sabrina is allowed to have me over once, with her father there, but Bianca says she must come to our house first to meet her.

"She seems loose," Bianca says after Sabrina leaves.

I don't know what that means, but I know it doesn't mean anything nice.

"What's that supposed to mean?"

Bianca doesn't like me questioning her, but I think I have a right to know why she says the things she does about my friends.

"The way she dresses… those pants," her face scrunches up. "I don't want you going over there."

"Parachute pants? That's what all of the kids in school wear."

"She looks like a French whore."

"What does that mean!" I yell and cry. How dare she call my friend such an undeserving name! I do an about face and stomp right into my room.

Bianca doesn't like any of my new friends; she is just as judgmental and picky about the kids from church. She is starting to get that way about me, too.

*   *   *   *   *

"You need to wear your robe," Bianca announces.

"You mean over this?" I question, tugging at my long shirt.

I am wearing an old, red, oversized t-shirt nightgown she'd given me last year. It hangs on me like a potato sack, right past my knees.

"Yes," she says. "I can see your nipples."

"How? You can't see through it. I can't see through it. It's thick like a shirt."

"I can see the outline of your nipples. Go put a robe on. You can't be walking around your dad like that."

It is over 75 degrees, and I'm not allowed to wear a t-shirt?

"But it's hot," I whine.

"Susanna!" she snaps. "Put your robe on or go to bed now!"

Dad is in the other room on the computer.

Why doesn't he defend me at all? I'm not doing anything wrong! This is ridiculous!

I am starting to get sick of Bianca's weirdness with everything that I do. I decide to go to my room instead of look at her. I pull up my sleeves and pick at my arms for the rest of the night.

* * * * *

Over the summer, right after I moved in with Dad and Bianca, she paid me $5 to mow our lawn and another $5 to mow the neighbor's lawn across the street. Bianca used to mow it herself but said she figured I needed the money to buy myself some things, and she thought it was a good idea to learn how to earn money. I was happy making money, even though I hated mowing lawns.

The neighbors across the street were snowbirds that were gone most of the time, and their lawn grew quickly after only a few days. It was so hot outside in the middle of the Florida summer afternoons with the heat index reaching to one hundred degrees or more that I felt as if I would pass out. The lawns were large, and since I had to bag all of the cut grass after only a few rounds up and down the yard, each took about an hour and a half each. After about a month I saved up $40.

Then Bianca stopped paying me to mow our lawn, and eventually stopped paying me to do the neighbor's .

"If you're not going to pay me, then I don't want to do it anymore. Why should I?" I tell her.

"You get out there and mow those damn lawns right now! We provide you with everything you need. This is your payment for what we have to buy."

"You mean my school supplies?"

"Like your new bra and the uniform for gym class," she tells me.

"Why do I have to pay for my own bra and gym uniform by mowing the neighbor's lawn? It's not ours. It's your job."

"Susanna! I said it's your job, and that's final!" she screams.

I stomp outside and kick the long grass around.

Bitch! Why do I have to mow the neighbor's lawn? I don't even know them!

While I do all of the work, Bianca keeps the money the neighbors give her for mowing their lawn. I find out something else - the neighbor has been paying Bianca ten dollars to mow their lawn the entire time!

What a bitch! I've been robbed!

It's time to mow our lawn again. I am not happy because Bianca has gypped me. I start at the very back of our yard, right where Bianca has just planted her new flowers. They are still small, maybe six inches, and haven't bloomed all the way yet. It is more work to go around them than to do what I had in mind. Pretending I don't see them, I mow over all six new plants. It is my way of getting back at her for ripping me off.

I don't realize Bianca is watching me. She runs out of the house screaming like a banshee.

"Susanna! Susanna! What are you doing! Get off of my flowers right now!"

She slaps me across my arm. *Hard.*

"Stop hitting me!" I yell.

Dad is standing there bewildered. He doesn't realize what has just happened.

"Susanna mowed over my new mums!"

Dad starts yelling at me too, but I don't care. I am sick of her being a bitch to me.

Bianca is so upset I think she's going to cry, which makes me feel a little bad. But just a little. I think it serves her right for ripping me off, and she should mow her own damn lawns.

Chapter Ten
Forsaken

I don't like school very much. My history teacher is a weirdo. My math and English teachers hate kids. My science teacher is rumored to have a wooden breast and screams at us every day. And in my physical education class, a big brown-skinned girl named Tonya wants to beat me up.

I don't know Tonya, nor have I ever done anything to her. She's been suspended from school for things, and this week I am her punching bag. Tonya is twice my size, literally, in both height and weight. I dread going to PE class. Everyone else is scared of her, too, because of her size and loudness.

As I'm changing out of my gym uniform, I notice someone from behind coming at me. It is Tonya. She corners me in the locker room and pushes me around. She towers over me, holds up her fist.

"I'm going to punch you in your face!" she says over and over again.

"What did I do to you?"

I have never spoken to her. What is her problem?

My stomach knots. I shake. I cry.

"Leave that little girl alone," her friend tells her.

Everyone else wants to help, but they know that Tonya will beat them up, too. Our coach sees what's happening and puts a stop to it. Tonya gets sent to the principal and suspended. She ends up getting into more trouble and eventually leaves school. I am glad I never have to deal with her again.

*   *   *   *   *

The only classes that I enjoy are on The Wheel, which is four classes divided up throughout the year; a new one rotates each nine weeks. I had agriculture last nine weeks. I hated it. I'm not into tractors or raising pigs or farming. I didn't have friends in that class, and I didn't fit in.

This nine weeks I have shop, which seems to be everyone's favorite. The teacher is cool. We don't have to sit at a desk every day, and we're allowed to talk to our friends. The teacher shows us how to build things, like wooden boxes and signs. I love cutting wood, engraving, and using wood burners.

I like being able to build things, but most of all there is a boy named Cody Bogart that I like in the advanced class next door. He is two years older, and I have had a crush on him for a while.

He starts talking to me when my friend Emily tells him about the crush. He tells me to meet him by the bathrooms, which are right in the hallway between the two classrooms. He opens one of the bathroom doors and tells me to go in. I'm unsure of what to do or what he is going to do, and I don't want to get in trouble. He pushes me inside, comes in, and shuts the door behind him.

"You're going to get me in trouble!"

"No, I'm not. Come here."

He grabs me and shoves his tongue down my throat. It was gross, not a nice kiss. I quickly leave the bathroom. No one notices.

Cody walks out a few seconds later. Still, no one notices.

"Give me head," he says.

"What?" I ask.

"Give me head," he repeats.

"What's that?"

"You don't know what it means?"

I shake my head.

"Get out of here. You're just a little kid," he says. "When you find out you can meet me back here and give me head."

I find Emily in the classroom and tell her what happened.

"What does that mean?" she asks.

"I don't know. Let's ask some around."

One of the boys tells us what head means. Both Emily and I cringe. We think that Cody Bogart is a completely disgusting pig, and I don't like him anymore.

*   *   *   *   *

I have no life after school. All I can look forward to is a lot of homework and church. Church comes before homework. I am too tired to do both. My grades suck.

Clothes are a big issue for me. My preference has changed tremendously from last year. I no longer want to wear the cute frilly dresses and saddle shoes that Bianca buys. I want to dress like everyone else.

I beg for a pair of parachute pants.

"They're sleazy," Bianca says.

I beg for a pair of name brand jeans.

"They're a waste of money."

I ask for a pair of new sneakers.

"You already have a pair."

"They're ripped."

"You ripped them."

"They got ripped on the desk at school, and my socks are showing through."

"They're going to have to last you until next year."

I do my best to fit in with style, but it doesn't seem to happen. I don't even care if it has a name brand. I just want it to be something I like, not what Bianca picks. Some of my friends help me out and give me some of their hand-me-downs.

"Too tight," Bianca says about a pair of jeans that fit perfectly.

"Too revealing," Bianca says about a dress that covers my chest.

"Too worldly," Bianca says about a shirt with spray painted designs.

I walk home from the bus stop wearing a dress that I've worn all year.

"You're not wearing that dress anymore," Bianca informs me. "It's too short."

"But I'm wearing shorts under it."

"I don't care. It's too short."

"But what if I…," I attempt to ask her if I can wear the dress as a shirt over a pair of pants.

"Nope! You're not wearing it!"

"You didn't let me finish!"

"Susanna!" she screams, hitting me open-handed, smack dead in the center of my face, right on my nose.

I see black, stumble to the couch, stunned. My face stings. I feel my nose for blood and cry. I can't believe what just happened. I didn't deserve that.

"I'm sorry for smacking you. I thought you were talking back to me."

"I was just trying to ask if I could wear it as a shirt!" I say between sobs.

I don't know if she's planning to hit me again, but I am ready to put up a fight. I know when to have my guard up, and now that I've seen another side to this good Christian woman my dad married, I hate myself again.

Bianca agrees that it's okay to wear my dress as a shirt over a long pair of pants.

Since I no longer want to be near her, I go to my room and pick at my arms. I don't care how they look.

* * * * *

I visit Mom every two weekends. It's kind of strange and uncomfortable, but Marcus is a lot nicer than he used to be. It's the first time since he married Mom that he isn't being that big of a jerk. More than anything, I love seeing the babies. They're getting so big, and I miss watching them grow up.

The weirder Bianca gets, the more I like visiting Mom.

Babette, my best friend since kindergarten, is having a birthday party with a group of girls and boys from school. Even though her parents are going to be there, I'm not allowed to go.

"Boys will be there, and we don't know these parents. The answer is no," Bianca says.

"But I've known her since kindergarten. We were best friends for three years!" I beg.

How stupid that I can't go to my own friend's party!

"She's ridiculous," says Mom. "Babette 's been your friend for many years. So what if boys are going to be there? What does Bianca think is going to happen with her parents there?"

"She always thinks the worst with boys," I tell her.

"You can visit us the weekend of the party, and I'll take you there myself. Just don't let them know about it."

* * * * *

Unfortunately, thanks to Bianca rummaging through my notes to friends, my party visit is discovered. She must have done a lot of reading to find out, because I have two huge bags full of notes from the last three years. How dare she go through my things! It's none of her business!

Dad calls Mom.

"She wasn't allowed to go to that party and she knows it," I hear him say. "We told her she wasn't allowed, and you knew it, too."

I can't hear what Mom is saying.

"She's not allowed at any parties. Not while she's living under my roof."

I imagine that Mom told him off. Dad and Bianca talk about her after he hangs up the phone.

Bianca seems to know everything I do because she has no job and no life. She listens to my phone calls, and reads all of my notes to my friends and letters to my cousin Tracy.

Since Tracy and I write lengthy letters of ten or more pages at a time each week, we start sending our letters on cassette tapes instead. It's more fun and much easier to do than write. We exchange photos, songs and other memorabilia, and we probably say some things on the tapes that parents aren't supposed to hear.

Bianca is sneaky.

"What are on those tapes you have in your room?"

"Tapes?"

"The ones in your drawer that you keep."

"Music," I tell her.

"Just music?"

"Music and stuff Tracy sent me."

I'm not lying, so how can I possibly get in trouble?

"Let's listen to them," she says.

My stomach knots.

"Why? It's just my cousin talking to me about school and music that you don't like."

I figure maybe I'll get in trouble for listening to Prince and Billy Idol instead of holy music.

"Well I want to hear it," she says. "I want to hear what your cousin Tracy has to say, what you two have been saying back and forth."

I have to do something, anything to avoid letting her listen to any of those tapes. They are private. I don't want Tracy getting in trouble, and I know that at least one of her tapes says some personal stuff. The tape I am still working on is there, too. Did I say anything bad on it? I think quickly.

"I don't feel like it right now," I tell her. "I have homework."

Bianca leaves it at that. Am I safe?

I pick.

After dinner we sit on the porch.

Bianca brings up the topic of the tapes to Dad. Uh oh. Bianca already heard the tapes! There is no way dad cares about stupid tapes that kids make. He doesn't care about anything I do, unless I'm getting in trouble for something. My stomach knots. I want to throw up.

"Oh? Let's hear what your cousin Tracy has to say."

"No, I don't want to. It's personal," I tell him.

"Well, I can tell you I've already listened to them," Bianca admits. "It's a bunch of garbage. Your cousin Tracy is a whore! And we're going to be giving her parents a call later."

My heart sinks. My throat tightens. I feel like I'm going to have a heart attack. I want to puke. How dare she call my favorite cousin that name! She hasn't even met her! It's none of Bianca's business to hear anything my cousin has to say.

"What do you have to say on your tape?" Dad asks.

"Nothing much, mostly about school," I say.

"Then let's hear it," he demands.

"No!"

I'm stubborn. I tear up.

"Why not? Is there something on those tape you don't want us to hear?" he asks.

"No," I say, "I think it's my business to my cousin."

"Go get the tapes now or I'm getting the belt!" he threatens.

I know I'm in trouble now. I hate Bianca for butting into everything that I do. As I walk to my room to grab the tapes, I try to remember what the heck I said that's going to get me in trouble. I'm embarrassed, but I don't think I've done anything wrong. I open the drawer with the tapes. I grab them, jabbing my finger into the one I made, hoping to break it so they can't play it. I walk back to the porch and hand them to my dad.

"What did you do, try to break it?" he asks, examining the tape.

"No," I lie.

He messes with it for a few minutes, and manages to put it back together. Bianca puts it in the tape player, presses the play button, and turns it up loud enough for the neighbors to hear.

On the tape, I talk about regular things. And about how much Bianca pisses me off. I get in trouble for the language I use and not liking the way Bianca treats me. I guess I am not allowed to have feelings or privacy no matter where I live.

Out of the two-hour tape, there are only two or three things I say on it that they consider bad. Most of the tape is boring, even for me to listen to. Boring school, boring classes and boring teachers.

Then there is something I forgot. I talk about smacking Erick Mason's rear end because I have a crush on him.

"I can't believe you would talk that way and act like that!" Dad screams.

"Slllut!" growls Bianca, slurring the "sl" portion of the word to emphasize it.

I look at her like she's crazy. I know I am no slut, and the girls at school that are called that name do some really nasty things with boys. I have never done anything.

I don't care to listen to either of them anymore. I know there is nothing else on that tape that can get me into trouble. I know I'm not a bad kid; I am stupid for saying my feelings out loud. Almost two hours have passed, and Bianca announces that there isn't much else on the tape. Good. Maybe now I can go to my room.

"I have some things for you to read," she tells Dad.

"More?" he asks.

Bianca hands him some notes or letters; I can't tell which.

"Let's see what else you're doing," he says.

I sit on the porch couch in misery, my posture slouched. I don't think I have written anything as bad as they'd heard on the tape, and I don't think I can get in any more trouble than I already am.

"What's this mean?" Dad asks, showing me the letters and slash that read "j/k".

"It means just kidding," I tell him.

"What's this m/f?" he asks angrily.

What is there to be so angry about?

"My friend," I say truthfully.

His face turns red and he yells louder and angrier than ever, "No it doesn't! It means motherfucker!"

"No, it doesn't!" I scream back.

Tears stream down my reddened face, and I shake in fear and desperation of the outcome of all of this.

"It means my friend, and it even says it on it right there at the bottom!"

I point to the key at the bottom of the page.

How can he be so stupid? It says it in plain writing!

He continues accusing me of lying, like he always does when I tell the truth. I can't win anywhere. It is torture to sit and listen to him ask me every detail. By now I am screaming and crying because he keeps insisting that I am a liar. I am tired of all of the unnecessary drama that Bianca causes to make Dad feel sorry for her so she can receive more attention. Exhausted, all I want is to go to my room.

I get my wish; I am sent to my room for the night. I also get my radio taken away and my magazines thrown away. Worst of all, I am forbidden from writing or talking to my own cousin anymore. That means my summer trip to visit my family in New England is canceled, too. I am too tired to pick my arms, so I fall asleep.

Chapter Eleven
Addictions

Living with born-again Christians is just as bad as living with an alcoholic pothead. Although the two greatly differ in lifestyles from the outside, they play closely together in absurdities. Just as I am not allowed to have friends at Mom's house when Marcus is around, I am not allowed to have friends at Dad and Bianca's unless they're from our church. I am not allowed to do anything extracurricular, not even at school. Everything has to involve church.

I am not allowed to listen to any of my music unless it is by Christians, and even then Bianca has to approve of it because some Christian music is becoming "too worldly". I can't read magazines of my choice, never go to the movies, and I am not allowed to watch anything on TV unless it is a little kid's cartoon or on the Christian channel.

Bianca forces me to watch the "Praise The Lord" channel with Tammy Faye Baker crying her ridiculously painted eyes out and the boring 700 Club with mouse-face Pat Robertson. The only thing good about watching this crap is that it puts me to sleep. But I awaken to Bianca yelling at me.

"Susanna! Wake up! You need to watch this!"

I want to die. Kids don't like this garbage. It's fake and boring. All they do is ask for money and threaten people they are going to hell. Why couldn't she see that?

Bianca forbids me to have anything to do with unicorns or mythology.

"What's wrong with unicorns?" I ask.

"It's astrology! It's satanic! It's all devil worship!"

Bianca is so stupid she doesn't know the difference between myths and stars!

I am forced to live the life of a person that isn't me inside and accept things that I do not believe in. I have to pretend to be someone else in order to make everyone else happy. I am not happy at all. I have picked at my arms so much that I cannot wear sleeveless tops anymore.

Now that it's the end of the school year, I am ready to leave this life behind. Mom doesn't agree with anything Bianca forces me to do, and even Marcus acknowledges that turning everything into religion is crazy.

"They're nuts!" he exclaims, cigarette in his left hand, raising both hands in the air as if he is lifting his own self-esteem. "You're father used to be a fun guy and party all the time. Now this bitch comes along and runs his life!"

Marcus has changed his attitude towards me and says that I need to move back in with him and Mom. Coming from Marcus, I take this as his way of accepting and understanding me. It is the first weekend of my summer break, and I think it sounds like a good idea.

It seems to please my mother to call Bianca and announce that I am coming back to live with her and Marcus. Bianca takes it very badly and tells her that I am not welcome back in their home to live.

As if I want to go back there!

I watch the twins while Mom and Gramma pick up my belongings at the house. They are shocked to find that Bianca has thrown everything out into the front yard. They gather up everything, most of which has been literally thrown into boxes, leaving as quietly as they arrived.

Living back at Mom's is different from the last time, and it is definitely a different world from the last. Instead of moving into my old room that faces Scaggly's house, the twins and I switch because they are getting bigger and use two cribs instead of one. I am happy to be able to see them all the time again, and I think they are happy that I am back. In a matter of days, the twin's old yellow room is painted my favorite lavender. I am allowed to hang posters on my walls, read magazines, watch TV, listen to music that I like – and best of all, write to my cousin Tracy as often as I want. I am also allowed to visit her in New England as originally planned.

I look forward to other changes too, like getting a new hairstyle. My hair has grown out past my shoulders since Bianca's chop job from sixth grade, and I want a new look. I am ready to cut it off by my own choice this time and into a style that Bianca would never let me do. I cut my hair super short and buy myself some Sun-In.

Most of my summer days are spent helping Mom with the babies and sitting in the sun to bleach my hair. Mom lets me buy a new bikini after Bianca told her she had burned my old one.

I turn thirteen. Mom throws a small party with Gramma and Papa, her and Marcus, and the babies. I am happy to finally be a real teenager.

Because of the move, I have to change schools again. I recognize some of my old friends from Mrs. Esser's class, but they don't recognize me at first because of my new hair and makeup. I make new friends, too. Another new girl at school is Billie-Jo, or BJ, for short. We have most of our classes together, and now we're best friends. My other good friends are Jody and Lisa.

I have to walk through a very dark, seedy part of town to get to school. It's scary sometimes, especially being a small girl - and more so after Mike Riley ended up in the hospital when he got jumped for his wallet on his way home from school.

I am walking to school by myself this morning. It's humid out, even though it's only about seven o'clock, and I am already sweaty. The sun is still coming up. I try to walk with others, but there usually isn't anyone else around. An older dark skinned man in a pickup truck pulls up beside me. I don't look at him and keep walking, clutching my books tightly against my chest.

"Would you like a ride?" he asks.

"No thanks," I answer.

"Come on," he insists. "I'll give you a ride. Get on in."

"No," I persist, but he won't leave.

I think my heart is going to pound out of my chest. All I can think to do is run, and run fast, before I get kidnapped and disappear like the girl from my school did last year.

The man continues driving beside me. I run faster. All I want to do is get on campus where other people can see me. It is three blocks away, and I am already out of breath. The man finally gives up and drives away.

I am hysterical by the time I arrive at school. I look for my friends. One of them tells our principal, Mr. McCrary. I give him a description of the man and his truck, and he calls the company that the truck belongs to. No one knows who is in the truck, because the company no longer owns it. I am afraid to walk to and from school anymore, but I have no choice, because Mom doesn't have a car.

"Just run if someone comes up to you again," she says.

Luckily, a boy named Mike Nelson promises to walk with me most of the way home, at least until we are out of the dark part of town.

Finally, because of all of the violence and missing girls in the area, the school arranges for a bus stop.

*   *   *   *   *

I haven't seen my father since I moved out four months ago. He never calls me, and I'm not sure what to think or how to feel about it.

"Bianca runs his life now," Mom says. "He doesn't care about you."

Marcus repeats her. They repeat each other.

Bianca is pregnant now and has been busy decorating a room for the new baby. She is due around Thanksgiving. Bianca seems ecstatic that she is having a child of her own that she can mold the way she wants. I finally have a baby sister, and she is given everything that I have always dreamed about.

Since Dad must pay for my medical and dental care, Bianca finds the cheapest way to get around things. I have an open nerve on a molar. Bianca decides that my regular dentist charges too much, so she takes me to a really mean one that Dad went to as a kid. He had told me a long time ago that the guy was horrible.

Why would she take me to a place that Dad didn't like?

Dad is right about Dr. Browning. He is the worst dentist that I have ever met. His office is old like it is out of a 1940s mental asylum.

My first visit with Dr. Browning consists of his rough bedside manner, poking around the open nerve in my tooth. When I jolt out of the chair, he yells at me to stop moving. It is just like being in a real, live Stephen King novel. I leave crying and nauseated.

The next appointment doesn't seem so bad at first. Dr. Browning pokes around before permanently filling my tooth.

"How are you doing, nigger?"

What did he just say?

"Hmm?" I mumble through cotton stuck in my mouth.

"How are you doing, nigger? You're wearing your hair like a nigger." He emphasizes the "n" word with a slight scowl.

It is a word that I have heard before - at school and from my Uncle Charlie. I'm afraid of him touching me now because he might slip and gash my throat because he hates kids and blacks.

He fills my tooth. We leave.

"Don't *ever* take me back to that horrible man! I would rather pull my own teeth!" I tell Bianca.

I don't care if I get in trouble for being angry. I would rather kick that stupid old dentist right in the face if I ever have to look at him again.

When I arrive home, I tell Mom.

"He really said that? What a jackass!" she says. "You don't have to worry about going to him again. I'll take you to the dentist myself and send your father the bill. Screw that cheap bitch he married."

* * * * *

It doesn't take long for things to return to the way they used to be. Marcus resumes his old ways. His sketchy-looking eye routine is at it again, as well as his bossiness and craziness. And worst of all - the accusations.

The twins will turn two shortly before Christmas. Things are a little crazy in the house with them running around in different directions at the same time. Going anywhere with them is a huge challenge, and it takes two of us to control them.

Mom and Marcus go to dinner while I babysit. I play and chase them around the way I always do. Thomas falls onto the sharp edge of the baseboard against the wall and a huge dent in his forehead starts to swell like an egg. I am scared he is going to be brain damaged or die. I call the ambulance. The paramedics arrive. Thomas clings to me. Luckily, it turns out to be a bad bruise and a small scratch. The paramedics say he'll be fine, to put ice on the bruise, and don't to allow him to fall asleep for another couple of hours. They tell me I did the right thing by calling them.

Because I am not allowed to let Thomas go to sleep, the babies are still awake when Mom and Marcus arrive home.

"Why aren't the kids in bed yet?" Marcus growls.

I tell them what happened to Thomas. Marcus accuses me of not watching the boys.

"Yes, I was too watching him! I saw him fall. I watched it happen." I tell him. "I was right behind him."

"Well, you need to keep a better eye on them. This could have been serious," he scoffs.

"I was right there, they were running when he fell. It was just like the time Taylor fell and hit his head right in front of everyone at the restaurant."

"They're always running and hurting themselves, Marcus," Mom tries to stick up for me. "Taylor did it when the whole family was watching him."

"She needs to be more careful," Marcus grumbles. "She doesn't watch them close enough and she shouldn't let them run around."

"Let's not start, Marcus," Mom begs him. "We had a good night out. Susanna, just go to your room. I'll put the babies to bed."

Taylor clings to me.

"Sanna put to bed," he whines.

Taylor clings to me more than Thomas and never wants his own father near him.

Mom and I go upstairs together and put the babies to bed. The twins are noticeably all upset again, even after all of the work it took for me to calm them down after the paramedics left. Marcus has a way of upsetting all of us all of the time.

Taylor clings to my neck, inertly knowing that I will always be the big sister he can cling to when he needs someone. Thomas, in Mom's arms, seems more ready for bed.

"Nigh-nigh," we say to each of them, hearing Marcus crack open another beer downstairs and light another cigarette.

"I didn't do anything wrong," I cry to Mom in the baby room.

"Don't worry about him," she whispers. "We had a good dinner but he's had a few drinks. You know how he is."

I keep silent, feeling sorry for the boys for having to grow up with such a jerk of a dad. Mom quietly shuts the baby's bedroom door and goes in her room to change into her sexy nightly clothing. She joins him downstairs.

"I guess we can't go out anymore since Susanna can't watch them," I hear him say.

"Let's not talk about it anymore," I hear her say.

I stay in my prison room for the rest of the night with the door shut. I pick at my arms while listening to him fight with her about me not watching the babies properly.

*   *   *   *   *

I never understood why my mother married Marcus. Everyone else says she can do much better. She is smart and attractive and comes from a family of decent middle class people.

Marcus is quite the opposite: unattractive with ugly hair and a big fat nose and squinty eyes. I guess my mother liked his dark-skinned, toned body when she met him. Maybe if he wasn't such a jerk, he might be more attractive.

Mom quit her nursing job when she married Marcus because of his jealousy. He wanted her all to himself, and he didn't like that she worked around doctors. Anyone that has a job better than that of a garbage man is a snob in Marcus's eyes. He says she doesn't have to work, even though they always complain they don't have any money. Mom stays at home now. She didn't get pregnant with Taylor and Thomas until she and Marcus were married for a while.

Marcus is jealous of any man Mom speaks to, so she quit speaking to a lot of people – including most of her friends. The only friend that is still in her life is her best friend Sharla from high school. We escape to Sharla's house when things get too rough at home with Marcus, like the times when he drinks too much and pushes her around and she's all bruised up the next day. The last time we went to Sharla's was when Marcus did just that, and Mom said she wasn't going to take it anymore. As soon as Marcus left the house for work we packed up the baby's stuff and left. Sharla lives out in the middle of the woods, so we figured Marcus would never find us there. Each time Mom heard a motor she tensed up. Spending a night or two like that was no way to live.

Sharla told us we could stay as long as we wanted until Mom could find another place. Even though Mom said she was scared that he was going to find us, she broke down and called Marcus, and we went home the next day. She didn't seem to like being away from him for very long. I had hoped she was going to be done with him once and for all. I don't think I was the only one. I think Sharla mostly stopped talking to Mom after that.

The only other friend Mom has is Francesca. She's our next-door neighbor that lives with the biker. I think Mom is friends with her out of loneliness. Francesca's boyfriend looks like he was just released from prison, and I heard he smokes crack. Marcus is friends with him, and all of them party together.

Besides the neighbors there are only a few other friends they have, like the couple who had a baby the same day the twins were born and the other couple who has a baby with a big head. But it seems like all of their friends come and go in and out of their lives quickly.

*   *   *   *   *

I dive into my schoolwork as much as possible. English is my favorite class. But there is one boy I hate, because he always picks on me. Richard Raynard gets on my nerves every single day. He always gets in trouble in class, and he always finds ways to get others in trouble. He sits across the room from me, which means that I have to look at him and his skinny bird legs everyday. He and his blond, skinny surfer friends point and laugh at the clothes I wear - but Richard is the worst one of all. I am sick of his teasing and his making weird faces at me with his goofy braces, so I flip him the middle finger.

"Mrs. Merritt, Susanna showed me her middle finger," he tattles.

"If it's in her, it's going to come out of her," Mrs. Merritt tells Richard, her coke-bottle thick glasses making her eyes seem huge. "Because whatever you put in something has to come out somehow."

Luckily, I don't get sent to the office for that.

Unintentionally, I knock my pencil off of the chair desk. As I reach over to pick it up, the chair's legs give out and slide across the terrazzo floor. I land on my side, my hip hurting from the edge of the desk gashing into me, but I hold my composure and try to laugh along with the rest of the class. I am learning to laugh at myself so they don't pick on me as much.

Mrs. Merritt, thinking I am clowning around and fell on purpose, yells at me and threatens to send me to the office. I am already embarrassed, but everyone sticks up for me and tells the teacher I didn't mean to do it. It isn't so bad until Richard Raynard announces to the class that my face is as red as my underwear and that he saw up my dress when I fell over. Mrs. Merritt sends him to the office, and even though my side still hurts, I laugh to myself that Richard got in trouble for being a jerk to me.

Since my math teacher thinks I am doing so well in pre-algebra, he suggests that I move to regular algebra. That proves to be a mistake because I am lost. Pre-algebra didn't seem like much of a challenge at first, but I haven't learned enough of the basics to understand regular algebra. Although the teacher calls Mom and explains that I am really struggling, and it is his fault for suggesting the advancement too soon, Marcus punishes me for receiving a "D" on my report card. That means I'm not allowed to do anything until the next report card – in nine more weeks. That means no TV, no music, and no friends. It doesn't matter how much the teacher stands up for me; Marcus is determined to remain a jerk.

The only thing I am allowed to do related to school is participate in our school's chorus competition in Tallahassee. Our chorus teacher, Mrs. Malabou, picks the ugliest dress pattern that anyone can imagine – it looks like it's from the 1800s. Since all of our dresses have to be hand sewn, Mom sews the floor-length, puffy red dress for the competition. Even though I like chorus, I don't like Mrs. Malabou much. She is an attractive caramel-skinned teacher who is mean a lot of the time.

If we are off key at all, she screams and makes us do stupid high and low "la la la" singing exercises. It's like being back at the Four Square church. She treats us like she expects us to sing and act like a professional group rather than a bunch of junior high school kids.

*   *   *   *   *

It is a chilly, but sunny afternoon. After gym class I head to history. I hear an annoying boy named John yelling in the courtyard.

"The space shuttle blew up!"

He points to the sky at a puffy looking cloud in the air. John is known to say and do things for attention, so I don't believe him.

"Shut up!" I say. "That's just a cloud."

"No, I swear!" he says.

John isn't lying. I arrive to history class. Our teacher, Mrs. Still, has the television on and announces that the Space Shuttle Challenger has exploded into the sky, killing all seven astronauts, including the first teacher in space. I have never seen a teacher cry until I see Mrs. Still. The entire class sits in awe as we watch the tragedy on the news for the entire fifty minutes. Mrs. Still tells us that it is an historical day in our lives, and that in the future we will always remember what we were doing on the day that the Space Shuttle Challenger blew up.

I transfer back to pre-algebra so that I can bring up my grade point average again and get off of punishment. Now that I have that problem resolved, I have another one.

Danielle, from my first sixth-grade class, moved to our school, and after I show her around and introduce her to some friends, she starts trouble with me. She tells other girls – bigger girls – that I am a slut and do things with boys. All of my friends are aware that I am not allowed out of my house and not allowed to date. Danielle has always been a liar, but I never thought she'd do something like this, especially since I did her a favor.

I notice a girl named Brenna giving me dirty looks. I don't know what to think of it at first, because I have never spoken to her. She never smiles; she scares people.

Within hours, a few other girls start giving me dirty looks. It seems like an entire clique hates me, and since I hardly know any of them, I can't figure out why. All that I know is that they have all known each other since elementary school, and I am still considered one of the new girls. The girls knock into me on purpose in the hallway, walk by my desk and knock my books off, flick me in the head, and elbow me in the side. They call me names out loud and laugh, but not loud enough for the teachers to hear.

My stomach is in knots. I go home and pick. I am afraid to go to back to school, but I don't want to be home, either. I hate my life. I hate myself now more than ever.

Brenna and her friend Lydia come up from behind me in the locker room while everyone is changing into gym uniforms.

"I'm going to kick your ass," Brenna breathes down my neck. Her tall body blocks mine. My back is to her; I ignore her.

Lydia stands behind her, smirking. Brenna has literally cornered me, demanding her attention. I know if I turn around I will have to look at her and smell her breath.

"I'm talking to you!" she raises her voice.

"I haven't done anything to you. Leave me alone," I barely mouth out of my tightened throat, still facing my locker.

Other girls watch. No one steps in.

"You wait until after school," she threatens me, glaring her eyes and snarling her lips, revealing the braces on her teeth. "I know you live in nigger town, and I'm going to kill you before you get home today. I'm going to miss my bus so I can kick your ass, so you better watch out!"

She slams my locker door shut with my hand still in it. I scream out in pain. I start hyperventilating. I truly think Brenna is going to kill me. It is bad enough having to walk home through an awful neighborhood, but now I have to worry about this mean girl purposely following me on my way home today.

Someone notifies the coach, and Brenna and Lydia are sent to the principal's office. The entire class tells the coach that I did nothing to provoke either Brenna or Lydia. The coach calls Mom and tells her that she thinks I should go home for the day because I am broken out in hives.

I arrive home and Mom inspects me.

"You don't have hives!" Mom snaps. "That coach doesn't know what she's talking about!"

I don't know what hives are, but my skin is all blotchy and red. It seems like Mom is mad at me for being sent home.

"What are you so scared of this girl for?"

"She's twice my size," I cry. "She's weird and everyone else is scared of her, too."

"She's not going to touch you. Just kick her ass!"

"If I fight back I'll get suspended!" I plead.

My biggest fear is getting suspended from school and having a record for it. Despite the bullies, I really like school.

"You don't understand. She has the whole school ganged up on me."

"What did you do to her?"

"I didn't do anything. She's just a bully, and Danielle has been spreading lies about me saying I do things with boys, and it's not true!"

I am upset all over again for the interrogation for something that I did not cause.

"You need to go to school and ignore her. You can't come home because of this anymore."

Even with Mom I can't win this battle. How can she not understand this? She'd told me once when she was beat up every day on her way to school by a boy, and her brothers had to rescue her. I don't have anyone to rescue me.

Brenna is suspended for a few days and Lydia leaves me alone. I am relieved she is gone, but I am petrified when she comes back. A bunch of my brown-skinned girl friends tell me not to worry, that Brenna won't bother me because she will have to go through them first.

BJ, who is friends with everyone, has a talk with Brenna and tells her about the stuff I am going through at home. Brenna says she will leave me alone and offers me a place to stay if I want to run away. I find out that the whole reason Brenna hated me was because of a boy that she liked that liked me. I hadn't even known.

Chapter Twelve
Boys

I am glad it's summer vacation again. I'm motivated to get a summer job, but I keep getting the same response from every place I apply: "You're only thirteen. You can't work here until you're fifteen - and that's only if you have a work permit."

But I am determined.

I finally get hired as a junior camp counselor at the Y, and even though I don't get paid, it gets me out of the house. It's only two blocks from our house, so I can walk to work. I enjoy working with little kids and going on field trips to places that I'm normally unable to go. I also meet new friends.

Two of them are a Puerto Rican brother and sister; both are in high school. Isamar scares me, but I have a crush on Carlos. Isamar is loud and rude, and often acts like a bully, even to the little kids she doesn't like. Our main adult counselor, Victoria, has cerebral palsy, and Isamar makes fun of her. On the days that Isamar isn't there, everyone is happy, including the other counselors and many of the children.

Like I do during a lot of summers, I spend a lot of time at Gramma and Papa's. Since my work is right near Papa's work, he drops me off at the Y in the mornings and picks me up from Mom's in the afternoon. I eat dinner with them, spend some time at the neighborhood pool, and head back to the house. I am happy.

Walking into the house still wet and smelling of chlorine, the air-conditioning freezes me until I dry off and change. The house has a leftover scent of Gramma's fried chicken, along with Papa's stinky after-dinner cigar. If *Sixty Minutes* isn't still on when I return from the pool, a game of *Jeopardy* or *Wheel of Fortune* is blaring from the television. Papa in his rocker, I join Gramma on the brown tweed couch, all of us playing along with the game shows and trying to guess the correct answers. My favorite part is Gramma always has coffee ice cream or my favorite brand of chocolate chip cookies waiting for me.

And then I meet Estha.

Her real name is Esther, but we call her Estha because that's how she says her name. She has a strong New England accent with all of her r-ending words with an "a" sound. Estha is spending the summer with her grandparents. She wants to be a junior counselor at the Y, too, because she is bored with her Grammy and Grampy.

It doesn't take us long to figure out that we can take the city bus to and from work instead of having to ride with Papa. Estha is fun and full of stories about all of the kids our age where she lives; they are nothing like my friends from school. Estha is funny in a sarcastic sense, having a unique way of making fun of people without letting them know it.

We are riding the bus from the mall, and some strange looking metal-head guy wearing a black t-shirt and blue jeans sits near us, listening to headphones.

"What are you listening to?" Estha, outspoken and unafraid to talk to anyone, asks him.

"O-O-O-Ozzy... O-O-O-Osbourne," he answers with a very terrible stutter.

Estha looks at me, her eyes widen, and I know she is going to burst out laughing.

"I've never heard of O-O-O-Ozzy. I bet he's g-g-g-good."

Her burst of laughter erupts. Even though I hate making fun of people, she makes me laugh.

One of the boys from work, Michael, goes to my school. Everyone says he likes me, but I'm not interested in anything more than being friends with him. Estha makes fun of his very noticeable profusely bucked teeth.

Michael asks me if I would like to go to a concert with him. At first I don't want to go, because I don't want him to get the wrong idea, but Estha talks me into it.

"Go Susanna! If he's paying for everything just go! You don't have to do anything with him. If he tries to kiss you with his teeth just turn your head," she says, laughing at her own joke.

I am given permission from Gramma and Papa to attend the concert because Michael's dad will be taking us and chaperoning. I am glad his dad is going to be there too, because there is less of a chance that Michael might try something stupid.

It is my first real, live concert – Loverboy and Dokken. I hadn't heard of Dokken before but I think they are good as I watch them perform, long hair slinging and guitars blaring. I'm more interested in watching the bands because I love music so much. I mostly ignore Michael the whole time and enjoy the music, but he keeps trying to hold my hand, wanting me to be his girlfriend. When I cross my arms in front of me to hide my hands and turn my face from him, he gets the idea.

At work, Michael finally backs off completely when he sees that I like Carlos, and Carlos seems to like me.

Since all of us are employees of the Y, we have free privileges to use the pool. After work, Estha and I meet up with Carlos and Scott, a teen lifeguard who works with us. Estha is dating Scott; he drives a nice, expensive car and lives in a big rich-people house near the beach. He spoils Estha by bringing her roses and buying her jewelry. He doesn't act like a rich snob, but I can tell that this is exactly the type of boy that Estha likes.

No one else is at the Y except us. Estha is making out with Scott, which is a little uncomfortable because those are things people are supposed to do when no one else is looking. She is a lot more experienced than me and has already had sex with a few boys.

Carlos and I flirt and get close in the pool, but I am too scared to do anything. Plus, I keep thinking that Isamar might beat me up if she finds out I am with her brother.

When summer camp ends, so do all of our summer relationships. And Estha goes back up north.

* * * * *

I take the city bus to the mall before school starts to meet some friends. We run into Trent from school. Trent and I used to look at each other in the hallway and pass notes, but since I was never allowed out of the house, nothing came of it.

Trent has been my boyfriend for about a week. My friend, Heather, lives in our neighborhood. Mom allows me to go to the beach with her just once. We take the city bus across the bridge and walk the rest of the way. We meet up with Trent and walk the beach.

Mom picks up Heather and I later in the afternoon. Trent holds my hand until we see Mom's car then he lets go so I don't get in trouble. Mom pulls up, and I introduce her to Trent, who is very tall and well built for his age. Mom doesn't say much about him except that he looks a lot older than fourteen.

Later, I speak to Trent on the phone.

"What did your mom think of me?"

"She didn't really say," I tell him, "but I guess she thinks you're alright."

"Do you think she'll let us go out on a real date?"

"I doubt it," I tell him. "I'm not really allowed to date or go anywhere at night. I was only able to meet you at the beach today because Heather was there."

Trent doesn't say much after that, and there is an awkward silence.

"Your mom is hot."

"Hot?" I ask.

"Yeah. For an older woman she's hot."

It am quiet. Trent must get the hint.

"But you're hot, too," he quickly adds.

"That's gross! She's my MOM!"

I am disgusted.

"You know what I mean," he tries. "That's a good thing. It means you're going to be hot like her one day, too."

It doesn't take much for me to dislike a boy if he says something stupid, and this is it for me. I promptly dump him.

* * * * *

I consider myself lucky to spend the night at Allison's for two nights before school starts. Her mom is gone at night - either working as a bartender or having affairs on her drunk, jerky husband, so we have the entire time to do what we want. We take walks around the block in the dark, watch MTV music videos and rated R movies, and stay up most of the night. Allison's mom still isn't home at midnight and doesn't seem to care what we do.

Allison's older brother, Jeremy, is at the house, too. He is sixteen, in high school and is getting ready to go to a Saturday night party. He seems to know much more than the boys I am used to meeting. I think he is cool, especially with his long hair and nice body like the rockers in the bands on MTV. He gives us beer and warns us not to tell their mom. It is my first time drinking beer. When I stand up my legs feel rubbery, and I feel a little lightheaded.

Allison falls asleep early. Jeremy and I get close; he kisses me. I can't believe someone so much older wants to kiss me! He knows how to kiss nicely, not like Trent or Cody Bogart shoving their tongues down my throat.

Allison finds out when she wakes up to use the bathroom. It is obvious she is not happy with me liking her brother.

"You just like coming to my house because of Jeremy," she accuses.

"I have fun with you too," which is a borderline lie.

The truth is, Allison is not liked by a lot of people. But I feel a sense of obligation to her because we've been friends for so long. Most of the time she's okay to me, but she quickly gets mean for no reason.

Shortly after my weekend at Allison's, Jeremy goes to jail. He stole something, and I decide that he probably isn't so cool after all.

The only other boys in my life are the ones in my fantasies. I love the musicians that most parents hate, and I have posters of them all over my walls. But I also like clean-cut boys, too – the college boys.

I put my favorite Bon Jovi poster next to my bed so I can look at Jon Bon Jovi every night before I go to sleep and when I awake. Those are the kinds of boys I like most.

Chapter Thirteen
Position

Right before summer ended, I turned fourteen. Things seem to be going well. Today is the first day of school, and I'm glad to be getting out of the house again.

At school, I no longer have the same types of issues with girls bullying me. But BJ has bad news. She's moving because the military is transferring her dad. She is my best friend in the world right now and knows more about me than anyone.

I still have a lot of friends, like Jody and Lisa, as well as new friends. Cassidy, one of the popular girls who was voted Best Dressed, gives me her hand-me-down name brand clothes. She says she's happy that I can wear them, because she used to wear rags before her mom married a doctor.

All of my academic classes are honors level except for math. Biology is one of my favorite classes, because we only have six students and most of us are friends. I make straight A's in my computer class and always finish my work before everyone else. I take French and join the French Club.

I enter the county foreign language competition, recite the first sonnet of "Sonnets Pour Helene", and win first place. I enter my hand-constructed cardboard model of a guillotine to demonstrate part of France's history and win first place. I am happy and proud!

I also join the Student Government Association and become a manager for the tennis team. Now I have an opportunity to become Miss Junior High in our school's pageant.

My friend Geena is an excellent dancer and choreographs a tap dance routine for me as part of the talent portion of the competition. She comes to my house after school and teaches me everything step by step. She loans me one of her recital costumes - a bright yellow and black polka dotted suit with fringed edges and matching gloves. A girl from some of my classes, Shayla, loans me her pretty pink lacey gown for the evening gown portion. My friend Steve agrees to be my escort.

Marcus makes a big sign for me with plywood and Christmas lights. Even though he's being really nice about me entering the competition, he makes it clear that building the sign is a huge job. No matter how much I thank him, I feel as if I will owe him the rest of my life for it.

Mom and Gramma come to watch the performance. Dad doesn't seem to care much about anything I do and doesn't attend or congratulate me.

Out of about a dozen girls, I win fourth place! I'm so happy and very proud of my hard work, I cry happy tears. Stupid Richard Raynard laughs at me after the pageant.

"Are you crying because you lost?"

"No, because I'm happy," I tell him.

He appears confused.

"How can you be happy? You lost!"

He tries rubbing it in, still laughing and showing his stupid metal mouth.

"I didn't lose," I look him straight in the eye. "I still placed, you jerk! You're the loser, now go away!"

"But you didn't win, you only got fourth," he rambles, his stick legs poking out of his blue and pink surfer shorts, and his stupid crooked teeth shining at me.

I want to kick his legs out from under him with my pink pump heels and punch his silver-yellow teeth out of his face. I refuse to let him steal my one brief moment of happiness with his meanness and stupidity.

* * * * *

Things at home are beginning to sour in a bad, bad way. Marcus's drinking has increased, and he gets more combative daily. He continues to accuse me of doing things that I don't do, and I am really getting sick of it all.

"Your grandmother almost choked to death today," Marcus says.

I look at him, surprised. I turn to look at Mom. She is looking away.

Is this a joke?

"What?! What do you mean?" I love Gramma and never want anything bad to happen to her.

"She went to drink a cup of coffee today and almost choked to death," he continues. "She choked on your rings."

"What do you mean?" I ask.

"Your rings, Susanna. You put your rings in the coffee cup and your grandmother almost died from it."

"No I didn't," I tell him.

Before I wash the dishes I take off my rings and place them on top of a shelf near the toaster and coffee cup tree in the kitchen. Someone must have put the rings in one of the coffee cups. It swear it wasn't me.

"Well, who did it then?" Marcus growls.

"I don't know who did it! Maybe you did it, maybe Mom did it, maybe Gramma did it herself and forgot! But I know I didn't do it! Why would I put rings in a coffee cup?!"

I am getting really upset. How dare he accuse me of yet another thing that I knew in my heart that I haven't done.

"You're a liar! You put those rings in the coffee cup. Why can't you admit it?"

"Because I didn't do it!" I scream, getting more and more angry at his absurd accusations.

"Well now you're grounded for lying again."

I look at Mom. She looks away. I cannot believe that she is allowing him to get away with this crap all of the time.

I wish he would choke to death!

I am betting that Marcus has been looking for a reason to ground me on purpose because I have done all of my chores, and all of my grades are good. But there is a fun school event I am supposed to attend next week, and he likes to ruin everything for me.

"Don't count on going to the banquet you have planned next week," Marcus announces, just as I predicted.

I knew it! He's such a jerk! He did this on purpose!

My friend Donavan, whom I have known since Mrs. Esser's class, is being awarded a letter for football at a sports dinner banquet, and I am his date. Mom gave me permission to go, even though I am not allowed to date, but this is an exception since it's for school and his mom will be there.

I purposely stomp up each step to my room - hard. Why bother trying to be quiet when I'll only be called a liar anyway? I mouth off silently to myself all the way to my room and slam my door.

I no longer give a shit. What is the point of trying to be so careful about everything, because no matter what I do – or don't do - I get in trouble. I don't know how much more I can take of this life in this house anymore.

Within seconds, I hear the footsteps coming up the stairs. I know they are the ogre's. Throwing my door open and bursting into my room with belt in hand, Marcus tries to make me turn around.

I refuse. I fight back.

"Get your hands off of me!" I scream, holding up my arms to guard him from hitting me.

He swings the belt at me, hits me in random places. I do my best to block him, but he is bigger and stronger than me. Besides, he has a weapon.

"Stop it!" I scream. "Stop it! I hate you!"

He shoves me onto my bed. I lift my leg up to kick him, but I miss. He gets one good smack with the leather strap that wraps around my leg. I want to break his nose just like the guys did that he fought with when Mom and Dad were still married.

"Get off of me or I'm calling the police!" I scream.

He leaves the room.

A few minutes later the back of my thigh has a welt; the next morning, a five-inch bruise. My gym shorts don't hide it.

* * * * *

I hate breaking the news to Donavan.

"But your mom already said you could go," he reminds me, frowning.

"I know, but they grounded me for something stupid again, and now I can't. My stepfather accused me of trying to kill my grandmother."

"What?!" His eyes open wide, face distorts in disbelief. "Are you serious?"

"Yes," I answer, telling him the story, excluding the leather belt incident.

"That's the dumbest thing I've ever heard! Do you think if my mom talked to your mom she would change her mind?"

"Probably not, and I'll probably get in more trouble if she tries calling," I say. "They never change their minds when I'm grounded."

*   *   *   *   *

I am in my room, picking. The phone rings. I cringe, thinking it might be Donavan's mom.

"Sorry. Susanna is grounded and she can't go anywhere," I hear Mom say after a short pause. "Nope, not this time."

Another pause.

"Well that's the way it is in our house."

The call ended.

"Donavan's mom just called," she informs me. "I don't know why it's any of her business to explain why you're grounded."

Donavan admits that he doesn't think my parents are very nice, and that his mother thinks my mom is rude.

"It's not like you did anything bad," he says. "I already bought the ticket and everything."

I feel bad about it all.

"Yeah, I know," I agree. "And I got in trouble for your mom calling last night. I told you how they are. Now do you believe me?"

*   *   *   *   *

I have to get out of here!

Obviously jumping out of the window isn't an option, but I have to do *something*! Taking a handful of vitamins apparently isn't an option, either.

If I run away, where I will I go? Maybe I can find an old empty building and live there by myself. But how will I eat and shower? I remember Brenna's offer.

"You can stay at my house in my closet while I'm at school," she tells me. "Don't let my dad hear you."

I take what I can fit into a backpack and leave for school. The plan is to ride the bus home with Brenna after school and live at her house. I write a note to Mom and leave it on the kitchen table.

Dear Mom,

I can't stay here anymore. You don't have to worry about me anymore because I'm not coming back.

Susanna

I don't want to dismiss school, but I have no choice. Brenna will bring my homework to me until we can figure something else out. Today will be my last day.

"Susanna," Mrs. Merritt says. "You're wanted in the office."

My stomach sinks. My throat knots. My heart pumps faster. I know what this is about. Mom must have called the school looking for me. I walk into the office and speak to the lady at the front desk.

"Your mother called us and she's very concerned," she says. "She said you wrote a note that you are running away?"

I look at her. Blank. What do I say?

"Were you planning to run away?"

"Yeah, but I don't want to miss school."

She breaks a small smile.

"You need to call your mom on the phone and let her know you're okay. She's worried."

"You can call her. I don't care to talk to her anymore."

"Miss Hartigan, *you* have to call your mother right now."

She is very stern. She hands me the phone. I don't want to call. I don't want to speak to her at all. I know I'm in more trouble. I reluctantly make the call.

"It's me," I whisper. "I'm at school."

"What is this now that you're running away?" she starts.

"I changed my mind," I lie.

"You're to come straight home from school. You won't be going anywhere, you hear me?"

Yes, I hear her loud and clear, yelling in my ear.

I hang up. I really hadn't changed my mind, but now the principal is going to watch me get on my bus.

I ride my bus after school, contemplating the hell I have waiting for me when I get home. I'm the only one getting off at my stop today. Good. I don't feel like talking to anyone.

Maybe I'll throw myself in front of a car.

I try to figure out how I can do it just right.

Maybe in front of a big truck?

I can pretend I'm crossing the street and jump out in front of it. It will have to be going really fast so it does the job right.

No matter what, I still don't want to go home, and I still have a few blocks to walk. Do I really want to jump out in front of a car?

I see a pay phone. I pick it up and dial a hotline. A woman answers.

"How can I help you?" she asks.

"I don't know," I tell her, unsure of what to say.

"Are you thinking about hurting yourself?"

"Yes."

"What is going wrong with your life?"

"Everything."

"Like what? You can tell me because this is anonymous and I don't know you, and you don't know me."

I fill her in on some of everything.

"How old are you?"

"Fourteen."

"Have you thought about how you would hurt yourself?"

"I'd throw myself in front of a car."

"What would stop you from doing that?"

I thought about how I could cause a serious accident and still live, and then I'd really be in trouble.

"I'd miss the babies. Plus, I wouldn't want anyone else to get hurt."

Talking to her makes me feel a little better.

"I have to get home before I get in trouble for being late."

I hang up and walk home.

Mom nags that we have a great home and that other kids are abused, and I should consider myself lucky.

I tune her out and go to my mostly-empty room. I sit on my bed facing the big mirror above my dresser. I hate what I see. I pull my hair as hard as I can and scream into my pillow at the top of my lungs. I hate myself now more than ever.

* * * * *

Still pissed off at everything that has recently transpired, I decide that I don't give a damn what happens anymore. Maybe he will kill me. I don't care, because anything is better than living in this hell.

I clean the house and notice Marcus's generic cigarettes laying on his table. A few times the babies got into his pack and mashed them up all over the floor. I thought it was funny until they were given spankings.

I am pissed at him for being an asshole and having to inhale his stinky smoke all of the time and having to smell like smoke, thanks to him. I count five left in the pack, and I squeeze it hard enough so that they all break at the filter. I throw them down, missing the table.

Less than an hour later I am summoned from my room to confront the prick downstairs.

"Did you break my cigarettes?" he asks.

"No," I lie.

He opens the pack to show me. I stare. Blank.

"Susanna," Mom starts, "did you break Marcus's cigarettes?"

"No," I lie.

"Then how did they get broken?" Marcus snarls, crunching up his ugly face, standing with his fat ass in front of his recliner.

"I don't know," I lie, straight faced. "Maybe the babies did it."

"The babies didn't break my cigarettes and put them back in the pack," he says, gesturing his hands all over the place.

Oops. I hadn't thought about scattering them about the floor the way the babies would have done. But I didn't want the twins to get beat for it either.

He points at me.

"You did it!"

I know he knows I did it. But I don't care.

"Maybe I grabbed them too hard when I was dusting," I lie again, not caring one bit about consequences.

Why should I care? I'm be better off dead anyway.

"You opened the pack and broke my damn cigarettes!"

His voice rises more. I can tell that he is getting frustrated because he knows that I am actually lying for real this time. It is difficult for me to hold back the small bit of laughter that is waiting to escape. At the same time my heart is racing because I know I will get the shit end of the stick in the long run. But he is a jackass and deserves it.

I am sent to my room. Big deal. I don't want to have to look at his ugly, miserable face anyway. I walk up the steps with a feeling of satisfaction, go to my room, shut the door, and pick.

* * * * *

It's storming outside and freezing. Marcus is making me paint the ugly green stairwell a creamy color. I need to rinse the brushes, but it's pouring outside. I ask Mom what to do.

"You can rinse them in the sink. They'll be fine," she answers.

I begin to rinse, glad that I am done with this boring painting job. Not a minute later I hear the ogre's footsteps coming my way. He's been drinking all day. I cringe.

"What are you doing?!" he belches.

"Washing the paintbrushes," I answer.

What does it look like I'm doing, fuckface?

I know that he's going to accuse me of being a smart ass, and no matter what or how I answer I will be wrong. I feel the knot start up in stomach again.

"I can see that, smart ass!" he retorts. "Not in my sink you're not!"

Just as I thought. He is unbelievably predictable.

"Mom told me to do it."

Marcus uses his body to block me so that I can't get around him from between the wall and the sink. I am literally cornered. He reaches over me to shut off the water and tells me to take the brushes outside.

Mom enters after hearing the raucous.

"What's going on?" she asks.

I think she is annoyed with him.

"She can't rinse those brushes in the sink! She'll clog it up!" he barks at her.

"No she won't, Marcus. It's water-based paint. We rinse paintbrushes in here all the time. Even *you* do it."

"I don't want her doing it in the sink! She needs to go outside and rinse them with the hose."

Mom rolls her eyes, knowing he is impossible.

"It's raining out, Marcus!" Mom raises her voice.

"I don't give a damn! It's not raining that bad," which is a lie.

He turns back to me and growls, "You won't melt!"

It's one of his favorite insults, another subtle way of reminding me that I am a rotten person.

"Don't start, Marcus!" Mom pleads.

We are both used to his weekend rants and fits, always blowing up nothing into something. Every single weekend.

I want to throw up, even though I haven't eaten anything. All I want to do is rinse the brushes, shower, and read a book. I am clenching my fists, feeling my blood begin to boil. I am sick of him telling me what to do, how to do it, and treating us all like dirt. I am determined to stand here and do as my mother told me, as *she* pleases, not as *he* pleases. I am tired of *him* running every aspect of our lives!

Please, please, please save me Mom. Oh God, please, please, please, make him go away. I can't take another day of this.

I stand at the sink and continue rinsing the brushes in spite of his commands.

"Goddammit, Susanna!"

No more God's Hamlet, like I thought he was saying when I was a kid. He grabs the brushes out of my hands, splashing water and paint all over my face and hair.

"Get the hell outside and rinse the brushes!" he yells.

He starts to put his hands on me, but I am through with his bullying. I have one paintbrush in my hand and let him have it right across the face. I swing and kick, but I know I can't hurt his stupid, drunk ass. He almost loses his balance, which is laughable, but I am too angry to laugh anymore.

"Fuck you! Fuck you, motherfucker! Fuck you!" I scream louder than I ever have in my entire life. "Get the fuck away from me you fucking asshole! I hate you!"

I grab a wooden spoon and continue swinging at him to keep him away from me, hitting him over and over across the chest. All I ever wanted for the last seven years was for him to leave me the hell alone.

Marcus seems shocked that I am defending myself, but he is ready to fight me. He has red marks all over his chest in the shape of the spoon.

Good! That's payback for the welt on my leg! I hope it leaves bruises! I should break his fucking nose!

Contrary to her husband screaming the same words at me every day, Mom yells at me for the language I am using. The babies are crying. Taylor is more upset than Thomas at first, then they both cry.

"Now look at what you've done, you've got the babies all upset," he accuses.

"Fuck you!" I scream again. "You're the reason no one here is happy, you fucking fuck!"

I raise the wooden spoon at him again. We struggle. He manages to pry it out of my hand.

"Oh you think you're so tough, huh?"

He bows his chest up to me like a rooster. He goes to grab my face. I reach for the steak knives and he yanks me back. My adrenaline is so high that I am almost in a daze. Everything seems surreal.

"Get the fuck away from me or I'll cut your fucking throat!" I scream as loud as I can, hurting my own throat.

"See?" Marcus says to Mom. "Your kid is nuts!"

"Fuck you asshole!" I scream. "Stay away from me or I will fucking kill you!"

I scream at the top of my lungs once more before I run out the front door.

Although it is freezing cold and raining and all I am wearing is a thin pair of pants, a sweatshirt, and no shoes, I don't care. All I want is the hell out of that house and as far away from Marcus as possible.

I have nowhere to go, but I know I'm not going back to that house. I am scared to death of what might happen if I look back. It's difficult walking on the sidewalk, stepping on twigs and pebbles with cold, bare feet. I walk to the convenience store where the hookers hang out so I can use the pay phone. There are no hookers today.

I have no change for the phone so I enter the store and ask to use the phone to call the police. The clerk treats me like I am one of the druggies, saying no one is allowed to use the store phone and to use the pay phone outside. I am unaware that dialing 911 is free.

I tell the 911 operator the story and that I need to speak with Deputy Brockton, our school resource officer, since she is helping me deal with some of the things at home. Mrs. Still sent me to her they day that BJ made me show the teacher the welts and bruises on the back sides of my legs left from Marcus's belt. Deputy Brockton told me I could call her anytime I needed her. This is one of those times.

The lady on the phone connects me with the sheriff's department. I tell them I need to speak with the deputy, because she has helped me before. They say she is off duty, to call the local city police. I beg them if they could call her house, because she told me I could contact her anytime I need her. I sit on hold while they try to reach the deputy.

"I'm sorry, but she isn't answering her phone. I believe she's out of town for the weekend with her family and can't be reached. You're going to have to call the city police."

While waiting for the police to arrive, a man in a small red pickup truck pulls up to me and asks me something, but I can't hear him over the rain. I am lucky he doesn't try to kidnap me, like some of the other teen girls that have gone missing from the area.

"Wanna buy some rock?" he asks.

"Get the hell out of here, you idiot!" I scream at him. "The police are on their way here now!"

He takes off quickly, and I never see him again.

A few minutes later a city officer arrives. He is young and extremely rude. He tells me that most brats deserve to be hit and that I am probably one of those brats because I don't look abused. I inform him that my school resource officer is helping me out with this, and although I mention the drugs and alcohol, he doesn't seem concerned.

"A lot of people smoke pot. It doesn't make them violent," he tells me.

I thought police are supposed to help kids? That's what they teach us in school. I know that I could neither depend upon nor trust this stupid cop. I am stunned. I cannot believe that he refuses to help me. What do I do now?

"You just need to go home. There are worse calls than this I need to take care of, and I'm not going to interfere with a deputy's case."

The officer leaves. I stand helpless in the ice-cold rain, trying to hide under a tree for cover.

A couple in a car stops and asks if I need help. I think I can trust them, so I tell them that I need to call someone. They give me enough change to make two calls before driving away.

I call Jody, get her answering machine, and leave a message. I don't know what else to do. I had one more call to make, but to whom?

I am getting more and more desperate, because the temperature is dropping, and I am starving, and I have nowhere to go and only twenty-five cents in my hand.

Out of the corner of my eye I see Mom's car pull into the parking lot. The pay phones are on the other side of the lot, covered by trees where I am standing. I hide behind them, panicking and praying she doesn't see me.

Mom parks the car and I watch her enter the store. I wait, praying not to be seen. I watch her walk out of the store, get in her car, and leave. If Mom is in the car that means Marcus is home by himself. I'm definitely not going back to that house!

I use my last quarter to try calling Jody again.

Answering machine.

I stand around freezing for about an hour, afraid to go anywhere else because I don't know if Mom is still out looking for me.

Eventually I have to go somewhere. I am so cold I can barely move my toes anymore. My fingers are like ice sticks, and I look like a drowned rat. It is about forty degrees outside, and it's been about two or three hours since I left the house.

It hurts to walk, but I walk toward the house in a direction so that I am able to see who is home. I peek around a corner in case anyone is watching for me. I exhale. Gramma and Papa's car is in the driveway! I know Marcus will never do anything to me if they are at the house!

Relieved, but still reluctant, I go inside. Marcus the coward isn't here. Papa is here to pick me up and take me home with him and Gramma for the weekend. I am thankful. I feel as if there really is a God.

Chapter Fourteen
Papa

Mom has already filled Papa in on everything, but I am positive she sugarcoated it.

"I can't believe that language you used, Susanna. Where did you learn to use words like that?"

"Marcus says them to me all the time," I answer.

Why does this have to do with my language? What about what Marcus does to me every day?

"Is that so?" He looks at Mom.

She says nothing. The babies are standing nearby, listening.

"Well that's not right and it doesn't make it right for you to use them. It's not ladylike."

He is disappointed. I feel worse that Papa is ashamed of me than I do about cussing at Marcus.

"You're going to stay with Gramma and me for the rest of the weekend. I guess you'll need to get your things."

I walk to my room, almost feeling a sense of relief knowing that I won't have to look at Marcus for the rest of the weekend. I am still devastated by the turn of events, and happiness doesn't seem to be an option anytime soon.

"Jody has called here three times so you might want to give her a call," Mom says as we leave.

When we arrive at Gramma and Papa's, I am still wet and frozen. I'm able to take a hot shower to thaw out my body. It is comforting to know that I can sleep soundly in a place where there is no screaming or bullying.

I call Jody.

"What are you going to do?" she asks.

"I don't know," I say. "I don't want to go home."

"You can stay here if you need to," she offers.

I overhear Gramma and Papa talking about Marcus's drinking. They aren't aware of the drug use, and I am not about to tell them.

"That Marcus, he needs to stop his drinking," I hear Papa tell Gramma. "It's a disease. He needs to get help."

"I don't think he'll get help, Ralph," Gramma tells him. "But he needs to do something. This is getting out of hand now."

Gramma and Papa have no idea how much Marcus actually does drink. But I know. It is all that I've ever known.

"Marcus drinks all the time," I tell them. "Even in the morning."

"No, he can't drink in the morning before work," Papa disbelieves me. "Not with his job."

"Yes he does," I confide. "He opened a beer and put it between his legs and drove me to school everyday when I was in sixth grade."

Papa still doesn't believe me. I suppose he doesn't want to, because my mother hides it all so well. Maybe she isn't aware of the 6 a.m. drink, either, but she sees the rest of it all night long, every night of the week.

"Isn't that something?" Papa finally says.

"He doesn't need to be drinking that early in the morning. He has a problem," Gramma says.

"And driving. He shouldn't be driving with that beer in his lap. How does he work driving that big truck if he's drinking? He'll lose his job, then what will they do? He has kids to worry about for Christ's sake! He'll go to jail if the police pull him over." Papa stands in the living room, his hands on his waist, worried and disappointed. "Well what are we going to do now, Rita?"

Gramma shrugs her shoulders, disgusted.

"Nothing we can do. He has to get help, but I don't think he'll go. He's too proud for that."

* * * * *

Papa is an old-fashioned man who wears a suit and tie to work with a hat, even though he doesn't have to.

"It's the respectable way to dress for a job," he says.

Working as a tax collector, he takes off his hat when entering a building. When I was little, he brought me to his work to introduce me to everyone. The people he worked with seemed to love him, because he is a funny guy, they told me. But I already knew that.

"Your grandfather," one lady said to me, "he's a real character. He keeps us all on our toes." All of the other office people laughed and agreed.

Papa is probably the happiest person I know. He makes a joke out of everything, making people laugh everywhere, even at the dinner table. Gramma's vase in the center of the kitchen table became a toy for Papa at dinnertime; he'd hide behind it when I was small. When I tried looking for him, he moved the vase again. Now that I am older and big enough to see over the vase, I still pretend to hide.

Ever since I could talk, Papa played the face game with me. He put his hand over the top of his forehead and moved it down, creating a frown. Then he replaced it with a smiley by moving his hand from his chin in an upward motion. It's like a magic trick, but only Papa knows how to do it right. No matter how old I am, his funny face game makes me laugh.

While I stayed at their house when Mom worked as a nurse, Papa took me for walks to the railroad tracks, explained to me how trains worked and about the engineers that run them. On our walks he taught me how to spell big words like *hydrant* and *important*, so when I went to school I knew a lot of words that most kids my age didn't. When I was small enough to sit on his lap, Papa told me stories about the *Three Bears* and *Red Riding Hood*, and he told them in his story-telling voice, making each character a unique sound. He still makes me laugh with his funny voices and imitations.

* * * * *

To my dismay, I have to return home on Sunday evening. I am dreading every minute of it. The last place I want to be is anywhere near Marcus. Papa takes me home and says he is going to have a talk with Marcus about his drinking. I'm not sure how that will go over.

Marcus lies and says that I am making up stories, and that he only drinks one or two beers after work and he has some on weekends when he's watching a game. Marcus claims that I am a liar, and I exaggerate because I am a brat not getting my way. I shudder at the thought of Papa leaving me there to fend for myself without his protection. But he has to leave, and I am fearful more than ever, especially after having told on Marcus.

"I never drank beer before work," Marcus snarls at me. "I don't know what you're thinking. It was probably soda or coffee, but I never drank beer. Why did you tell your grandfather I was drinking beer?"

"Because you were," I say. None of his manipulation can convince me of what I know to be the truth, although since his games are so convincing, I begin to question myself.

"That wasn't beer," Marcus tries to play with my mind again. But I know what I saw. I am used to his mind games, and I am not going to let him fool me.

"Let's not get into it tonight," Mom says. "Susanna, just go up to your room and get ready for school tomorrow."

I gladly go to my room. Anything is better than having to speak to Marcus or deal with his issues. But I am also sick of being confined to my room just because Marcus is an ass.

* * * * *

Deputy Brockton calls me into her office when I arrive at school.

"What happened this weekend?" she asks.

I tell her the whole story.

"I'm so sorry I wasn't there for you," her forehead wrinkles. "I was camping with my family and had no way of getting any messages."

"I understand," I tell her. "There's something else though."

"What is it?"

"Well," I pause, take a deep breath and hesitate. "Marcus smokes pot."

Deputy Brockton's expression is more serious.

"To tell you the truth, that doesn't surprise me. Tell me about it."

I tell her about how long I have known about pot smoking, what I know about seeds and papers, joints and bongs, and the little silver tray that Marcus uses to roll his joints.

She asks if I've seen other drugs, and I tell her that I haven't but I know our biker neighbor smokes crack.

"Do your grandparents know about this?"

I shake my head.

"Do you want me to tell them?" she asks. "Or would you like to?"

I shook my head in fear. "No, I'm definitely not going to tell them."

Deputy Brockton makes an appointment with Papa, and he is sitting in her office when I'm called out of history class. She explains to him what I've told her.

"Now I don't know if I believe that," Papa says, glancing at me. "That's a little far fetched. My daughter was a nurse. I know she wouldn't do drugs. She knows better than that."

"I'm not making it up. I wouldn't lie about it," I say.

"Have I seen them do it? How would I know if I've seen them do it? I have never been around drugs in my life. That stuff wasn't around when I was growing up, but if it was I never saw it."

"It's a very distinct odor," the deputy explains, "and you can't mistaken it if you smelled it. What Susanna has described isn't something that a kid can make up unless she's witnessed it."

"Well I'm going to ask Marcus myself. I'll know if he's lying to me."

Oh no! This won't be good! He's going to confront Marcus and I'm going to be stuck in the house absorbing his wrath!

Papa thanks the Deputy and leaves. I go back to class a complete wreck, dreading the future.

Papa doesn't get off of work until around dinnertime, so I nervously anticipate his arrival when I get home from school. No one else at home knows about his visit at school today. Not yet. I pick until I hear Mom.

"My father's here," I hear her say.

Marcus grumbles, hides his beer, pretends life is normal. My heart pounds. My stomach somersaults. While Papa and Marcus talk outside, I stay in my room. I hear Papa's car drive away. I hear Mom and Marcus talking, but I can't hear the words.

"Susanna, come down here," Marcus gripes.

Oh God! What is he going to do to me now?

I carefully walk downstairs, knowing that the night will not end well.

"Did you tell Papa that we smoke pot?" Mom asks.

She doesn't look happy. I can tell she is not on my side.

"No," I say.

It is true. I'm not the one who told Papa. It was Deputy Brockton.

"Then why did he ask Marcus that?" she interrogates. "I want you to tell me right now!"

"Because you're going to stay in your room until you tell us," Marcus chimes in.

As if I won't be there anyway.

"I don't know," I say, too afraid to reveal my source. I don't want them knowing I've been talking to the police at school.

"Bullshit! He didn't make it up, Susanna!" Mom accuses. "You told him we smoke pot, didn't you?"

"It's okay," Marcus interrupts. "I'll handle this."

I close my eyes, picturing how the night will end.

"I don't smoke pot. I roll my own cigarettes," Marcus continues as he pulls out his silver pot tray. This time he has real tobacco on it. I can tell the difference between brown and green; he is colored blind and cannot.

"See?" Marcus shows me. "See? You thought I was smoking pot. It's not pot. I roll my own cigarettes."

His voice cracking, he repeats himself about rolling his own cigarettes and pounds at the tray with his index finger as if to show me he is telling the truth. But I know better. He is a liar.

"It's just cigarettes, Susanna," Mom lies. "Did you think it was pot?"

She seems calmer now. She's also playing the game.

"Yes," I say.

"Well it's not," they both chide in stereo.

"It's not pot," Marcus repeats. "See, you thought it was pot, but it was just tobacco. I just roll my own cigarettes. I know they've been teaching you that stuff in school about just say no and all that, right?"

I nod my head. I blankly stare. I am tired of listening to the repetitive words and stupid lies.

"But I just roll my own cigarettes," he tries convincing himself of his own lies, nervous laughter ending each sentence.

"It's not pot," he continually repeats over and over for about twenty minutes until Mom finally tells him we all agree it's not pot.

Since they can't get any information out of me, I am sent to my room. I don't care, because I don't want to have to look at or listen to Marcus anymore. I'd rather pick my arms.

Chapter Fifteen
Pariah

Unexpectedly, I am called into Deputy Brockton's office again. She introduces me to a social worker from the Florida Department of Health and Rehabilitative Services. I don't know why she is here or why I have to talk to her.

"Susanna, by law I have to report some of the things that you've told me," Deputy Brockton says. "I'm going to ask you to tell Ms. Morrison about the things that have been going on at your house."

I am tired of repeating myself, and after what happened last night, I am tired from not getting enough sleep. I am tired of all of this. I don't feel like anything I say is going to make a difference anyway.

Out of fear of getting into trouble with the important-looking woman sitting in front of me wearing a suit, I speak. I also fill them in on Marcus's new tobacco tray. They look at each other like they know something that I don't.

Deputy Brockton also wants me to relay the story to the HRS rep about the time Marcus hit me with his belt that left welts on my leg. They thank me and send me back to class. I finally start to feel validated.

I arrive home from school. Mom won't look at me.

"Hi," I say.

She ignores me. I figure she is still mad about Papa and the fake pot tray. I go upstairs and enter my room. I open the door to see that all of my posters are ripped from my walls. My diary and some notes I'd written to friends were sitting on top of my dresser.

"Where are my posters?" I ask Mom.

"In the garbage," her face and voice blank, she stares ahead without flinching to look at me.

Heart pounding, stomach knotting, I go back to my room. I pick until it's time for dinner. They make me sit and eat by myself. There is so much tension, it's difficult to eat.

"We had someone visit us here today," Mom says.

I am puzzled.

"You told a deputy at your school that Marcus hit you and that we smoke pot."

I almost choke on my food. My throat tightens. My stomach is in so many knots I think I'm going to puke. I feel like running out the front door and never looking back. I had no idea anyone was going to visit the house and repeat what I said. I thought everything was confidential! I just started trusting them!

I begin shaking. I cannot swallow the food in my mouth, but I can't spit it out in front of them.

"How can you sit there and eat?!" Mom screams at me. Her voice starts screeching and her face is all red. "We told you that we don't smoke pot! Now you have some social worker coming over here! Do you realize these babies can be taken from us?"

This is all news to me, so I don't know what to say. The last thing I want is to get in more trouble. I wish I had thrown myself in front of a truck like I planned!

"The cops came over here today and raided us," Marcus starts.

Raided?

I'd heard of Marcus talking about drug raids and scared of being busted. I'm not sure I believe him.

"Yeah, they came over and raided our house looking for pot," Mom joins.

I don't trust her either since she is part of the game.

"The cops came to the house and searched the place looking for pot!" Marcus repeats, raising his voice. "Why would they do that unless you said something?"

Someone had obviously filled them in on what I said at school today, but I still have my doubts about any sort of "raid" claims.

"And you showed your teacher your ass?" Marcus squeals.

"What?!"

What is he talking about? I am so confused.

"You showed your teacher your ass in the bathroom!" He yells. "You told her that I beat you with the belt!"

Marcus walks closer to me, stands in front of me and gets in my face, "You think you've been beat? You've never been beat! You want to know what getting beat is like? My old man used to ball up his fist and punch us in the ass! Punch us! And you think you've been beat? You don't know what it's like to be beat but I tell you what, I wish I had beat you now!"

He paces the room, repeating himself over and over about getting beat.

"The teacher asked me what was on my leg!" I cry. "BJ told her and the teacher made me show her."

"I can't believe you," Mom says as if I betrayed her friendship. "Look at what you've done."

She takes her finger, lightly picks up the side of my plate, and shoves it across the table.

"How can you just sit there and eat?"

I sit, now unable to eat. I've only eaten a few bites and want to puke up every last bit. I want to disappear into thin air. I begin to pray that I will die soon. Who wants to live like this anyway? This isn't living. This is the HELL that the Foursquare Church should have warned me about!

Mom stands behind and over the left side of me the entire time she talks. I fear she's going to chop my head off with a knife or something, because I can feel her hatred at the back of my neck. Marcus stands on the other side of me. I am convinced the two of them are planning to kill me. I knew long ago that Marcus hated me, and now I know that my own mother does, too.

"Beat!" Marcus mumbles, laughs nervously. "Abused. You think you've been abused? *I've* been abused," his voice slightly higher, poking himself in the chest with his index finger as if to emphasize the *I*.

"You want to know what my father did to me and my brothers? He beat us and then he'd lock us in a hole in the wall for days and wouldn't feed us! My mother would sneak us food and one time he caught her so he beat her too! You don't know what abuse is!"

"I can't *stand* what you've done to us," Mom growls. "I can't stand *you*!"

I am right. She *does* hate me! She turns and walks into the living room. It hurts badly to hear her say that. She hates me as much as Marcus hates me, maybe more. I feel hopeless.

They both stand in the living room out of my sight but within perfect hearing distance. They're only a few feet away, and I can tell they are purposely speaking loud enough for me to hear them.

"Either she goes or I go," I hear Marcus tell Mom. "Unless she wants to go back to her school and tell them that she lied about the whole thing."

I lied? Fuck him! I did not lie, and I will not take it back!

"I don't care where she goes at this point," Mom answers. "But where can she go? Her father won't take her back. And we don't want her here."

"Let the State of Florida have her," Marcus says. "Let her go live with some foster family. See how much she likes that."

I don't care where I end up anymore. Why would I want to live with two people that hate my guts and tell me so? Living with a foster family sounds like a good option.

"You need to make some phone calls tomorrow and see about getting her into foster care," Marcus says.

I am still sitting at the table, doing nothing but staring at my plate, afraid to shift my eyes upward. I do not move. I trust no one. It's obvious I cannot finish my food. Who has an appetite with all of this chaos?

"Clean the dishes and get to your room," Marcus snarls.

"Don't bother with the dishes. I'll do the dishes. I don't want to look at your face for another minute," Mom interrupts.

I get up. Taylor has been listening and watching everything. Even at three years old, he seems to know how I feel. He tries to hug me, but when I go to hug him back, Marcus yells at me to leave his babies alone, that they are his kids and he doesn't want me touching them.

I go to my room and cry. As I pick, I think about what to do next. I'm only fourteen years old, so I don't have many choices. I can run away. I can kill myself. I can stay here and have everyone hate me. What kinds of choices are those?

I know that all I have is my self and my beliefs. Even if no one else believes in anything I say or do, I know in my own heart and mind that I am not the crazy one. I know what normal looks like, because things were normal before Marcus. Still hungry, confused, and exhausted from crying, I fall asleep.

When I awake, I can't wait to get to school so I can get out of the house. I get up and leave early so that I don't have to see anyone. I find Jody in the courtyard and tell her what happened last night. She is the only one that I can really talk to after BJ moved. It's embarrassing to talk about these things with anyone else.

It's hard to concentrate in school knowing what I have to go home to, and I hate when the bell rings. But at least today is Friday, and Papa is picking me up after work, so I'll spend the weekend with him and Gramma.

After school, I carefully enter the house, paying close attention to being unheard, turning the doorknob just right to do so and shutting it without making a click.

Just as Marcus does, Mom doesn't look at me or speak to me, even after I say, "Hi."

I hug the babies. Their innocent baby eyes tell me a lot.

"Hi, Sanna," they whisper. I hug them both.

Why are they whispering?

I tiptoe to my room, trying to be unheard and unnoticed. I open my door, and I can't believe my eyes. There are three boxes sitting on my floor. Everything I own is packed in two large boxes and one small one. I sit down on my bed in disbelief and swallowed hard.

What is going on? Where am I going? Am I going to a foster home?

I haven't spoken to my father since Christmas, so I know I'm not going back there. With no one informing me what is happening, I can only fear the worst. Is this another part of the game? I pick at my arms for about an hour until I hear Papa's car pull up.

"Where's Susanna?" I hear Papa.

"She's in her room," Mom says in her typical sullen mood, one that I have come to know quite frequently.

"Susanna!" Papa calls, always chipper.

Thank God! I can escape this hellhole for an entire weekend!

I walk downstairs with my small bag, happy to see Papa but still confused as to why my things are packed.

"Hi Papa," I say.

"You ready?" he asks.

"Yep."

He doesn't know. He doesn't even know about what's upstairs!

He can tell something is wrong. There is always something wrong here.

As we were about to leave, Marcus announces, "If you take her with you this weekend, you're not bringing her back on Sunday."

Papa is a little hard of hearing and asks Marcus to repeat himself.

"If you leave here with her, she's not coming back."

"What do you mean?" Papa asks, taken aback, his pale face red and posture defensive.

Papa is not one to get upset easily unless there is a good reason.

"She's not welcome back, just like I said," Marcus states matter-of-factly.

I have never heard him speak to my grandfather in that tone.

"I don't care what you do with her, but she's not welcome back in this house. Her father doesn't want her, the State won't take her, and we don't want her either. So if you take her, don't bring her back on Sunday because she won't be allowed in."

Marcus has a smirk on his face as he sits in his ugly recliner with his feet up in front of the TV, beer hidden away in a kitchen cooler ready to be cracked open at our departure. Papa is angry.

"Now what the hell are you talking about, Marcus? She lives here! This is her home. What do you expect me to do with her?"

Marcus lights a cigarette, and with his pompous attitude and sarcastic facial expressions, throws his hands in the air and says, "I don't care anymore."

Papa looks at my mother, shakes his finger.

"What the hell is he talking about?"

I have never seen my grandfather so mad in my life.

"To tell you the truth, I don't want her here either, Dad," my mother says, shrugging her shoulders.

"Oh come on! You two have lost your minds!" Papa's face gets even redder.

I am standing, not knowing what to say or do. I am nervous, and all I want to do is leave. I feel like throwing up.

"Let's go," Papa says to me.

"We'll talk about this later," he says to them.

"No," Marcus tells him. "This is it. I'm not talking about it anymore. If she stays here I'm leaving your daughter."

Papa is so mad that I am afraid he will have a heart attack.

His Irish face still red, he yells and points to them, "You people are ridiculous!"

We get into the car. Papa is still stewing.

"What is the matter with them two?" Papa asks me. "You're not a bad kid. I don't understand what it is that Marcus has against you."

"I don't know either, Papa. He's always been that way towards me since I was little but just not in front of you. You have no idea."

The ten-mile drive to his house is fairly quiet. When we arrive, Gramma knows something is wrong because Papa isn't his usual self. I walk to their back room where I always stay to spend the night. It doubles as a spare bedroom and Papa's office. I hear Papa telling Gramma what transpired at the house.

"What the hell is wrong with him?" I hear Gramma raise her voice, flustered. "What the hell are we going to do?"

"Well she's going to have to live with us because she has nowhere else to go."

"She can't live here. They won't allow it in this park. It's for adults only."

"Well, Rita, there isn't much choice. She can't stay at her father's, and Marcus said she's not allowed back to their house. She's probably better off living here anyway until he gets his booze under control."

"Where is she going to stay, Ralph? We don't have the room."

"We're going to have to figure something out. I'll have to give her my office and move the desk into our room. We'll figure something out."

I feel guilty that my grandparents are arguing over whether or not I am going to stay here and what they are going to do with me.

Gramma comes in the room. I've been sitting on the bed, picking while listening to them.

"I guess you're gonna have to stay here," she says, wiping the sweat off her brow. She looks stressed, but I can tell she isn't trying to blame me.

"Okay," I say.

I don't know what else to say. I feel like a burden to everyone, but I know that they don't want me to feel that way.

Being unwanted by your own parents is a terribly empty feeling.

Chapter Sixteen
Foundation

I know now that Papa believes I hadn't been lying about things.

"As sloppy as Marcus is about everything, he showed me that tray you were talking about and it was all cleaned up and neat," Papa tells me. "And I said to myself, 'why in the world would he keep that so cleaned up but not care about anything else?' And that's when I knew he was lying."

I am surprised to hear Papa's thoughts.

"He leaves his dirty clothes on the floor and his beer cans lying around for your mutha to clean up," he says in his Yankee accent, not pronouncing his r's so that "mother" sounds more like "mutha".

"His cigarettes a mess in the ashtray," Papa continues. "So why would he have such a nice neat tobacco tray? I asked myself that and I didn't believe him. I believe you were telling the truth, Susanna."

I am relieved.

"But your mutha…Your mutha. I don't understand at all. How she can live with a man like that. How she gave up being a nurse with all of that school she accomplished. Of course she has the babies now but before that she didn't. She could have married a doctor. But instead she married a garbage man that drinks."

I am surprised to hear Papa's feelings towards my mother.

"She was a nurse and she should know better than to do drugs," he continues. "I never understood drugs. My fatha was an alcoholic, you know, and because of that I never drank. But drugs, I don't see the point. They ruin people's lives. They become bums."

Papa's voice fluctuates up and down, especially down when he repeats words like "drugs" and "bums".

* * * * *

Living with Gramma and Papa is an entirely different world from living with Marcus or Bianca. I can breathe again without anyone judging me. Papa is strict about a lot of things, but I don't care. I feel safe with them. I know that no matter what, they will always love me.

Things have happened quickly and are going at ease with the new move. We manage to squeeze my dressers into the small room and shove the single bed up against the corner between the far wall and the door. I take half of the closet to hang my clothes. Everything else I own fits into my dressers. Things are tight, but I don't mind. I collect some new posters for my walls and surprise Gramma one night when I show her.

"Who are those girls?" she asks.

"Those aren't girls, Gramma!" I laugh. "That's Bon Jovi."

"Bun who?" she says, sort of laughing.

I know she is kidding me.

"Bon Jovi," I repeat.

"I thought they were girls with all that hair and makeup."

I laugh with her. I know that Gramma doesn't understand rock music or anything past the 1950's, and that is okay with me. We laugh about things like that. She calls my music "raucous" and I call hers "old people music".

Since Gramma and Papa's house is out of my school's zone, I can't take the bus. Papa drives me to school each day before he goes to work, then picks me up at the library after school, where I do my homework.

My friends at school tell me that I am not my normal cheery self like I used to be. I don't know why. I guess maybe I am depressed because I know my mother hates me. But I don't want to talk to her, either. I resent her for what she had let her husband do to me. It is easier not to talk about them than it is to admit they are alive.

A boy named Juan starts talking to me at the library. I tell him that my grandfather will be picking me up soon, and I need to wait outside for him. Juan asks where my parents are; I tell him they're dead.

I do not see my father much, nor do I speak to my mother. I miss the twins more than anything. My mother comes over on a Saturday or two but I don't want to see her. I dread it.

"You need to talk to your mutha," Papa says. "She's your mutha, and the only one you've got."

I pout because she is the last person I want to ever speak to again. She comes over, doesn't speak to me in a normal way. She doesn't even act like she wants to see me. She is judgmental and rude, and I feel as if my space is invaded when she makes the babies run in my room and yell at me to wake up early on weekends. What right does she have? It's not that I don't want to see the babies; it's that I don't think she has a right to my life anymore.

A few times my mother had to come over to the house to spend the night with the babies because of Marcus's drinking and pushing her around. Even though her and I don't see eye to eye on things, I still love her and wish she will leave him – if not for herself, then at least for Taylor and Thomas. Everyone knows she can do better finding a man that isn't abusive.

* * * * *

I meet new people in my neighborhood and join up with old friends from elementary school.

Angela, one of my closest friends, introduces me to all of her friends. Angela is dating a longhaired boy named Jason who is in and out of juvenile detention. Jason plays guitar and loud heavy metal music, even harder than the stuff I normally listen to. Many of Jason's friends are just like him, but some are much older and have either dropped out of school or are already adults.

Most everyone hangs out at Jason's house because his mom, Ally, doesn't care if people are there. A lot of the time she is passed out on the couch after being up all night and sleeps through it all while most of the teens have parties. Except for me.

Ally loves me, and Jason always makes fun of me, calling me a "goodie two shoes" because I don't participate in their fun. Even if I want to participate I can't because my curfew is eight o'clock. Ally is a pseudo mom to me. She's about the same age as my mom but she understands me a lot better. I can tell her just about anything and not worry about getting in trouble for it. She thinks that my mom and Marcus are nuts.

Ninth grade ends, and Angela helps me get a job where she works. They hire people at age fourteen, and it's the only place in town that will hire me. It's my first real, paid job at a restaurant. I bus tables. My favorite part about working there is walking in and smelling the freshly baked cinnamon buns. The restaurant has an old timey piano that plays by itself; it's filled with rooms of antiques and things from the past. Most of the people there are pretty nice except one of the bosses that everyone calls Archie-the-A-Hole. I work there for about six weeks before I decide I hate the job.

    I put up signs for different odd jobs, like cleaning houses, mowing lawns, and babysitting for people in the neighborhood. One lady has me clean her house each week, and even though I think her house is disgusting, I like making money. She has lots of black hair all over her floors and bathroom area. I gag every time I go. She's a complete slob.

    Papa gives me $2 a week to mow the lawn, and I make another $5 apiece mowing a few of the neighbor's lawns once a week or so. I'm not too keen on mowing lawns, either, but I have a goal in mind because there are certain things I want.

    Since I manage to save a few hundred dollars over the summer, I am able to have more freedoms. I sell my old ten-speed that Dad had given me for Christmas in fifth grade and buy myself a purple beach cruiser. Angela likes riding bikes, and we ride to the beach, then buy ice cream before heading across the bridge to home.

    I make it a point to visit Nana each week, too, especially since Grampa died, and she is alone. I don't feel sad that Grampa died because he was such a jerk to everyone.

    Nana and Gramma got into a fight over a will and stopped speaking. I don't understand what it's all about, but Gramma says that Nana is giving everything to Grampa's Jersey family and not even thinking about her own grandkids.

    I visit Nana, she cries, and asks me why Gramma won't visit her. I don't know what to tell her. I hate seeing her cry and feel sorry for her.

    I see Dad once in a while, but I don't spend the night. I rarely spend an afternoon with him and Bianca after going to church, which still completely bores me to death. Bianca just had another baby, so most of the time I end up watching hours of all of the home videos she takes of the girls. One afternoon is all I can take of that.

A lot of changes are happening. Estha is down a short visit with her Grammy again, but this time she is five months pregnant. It's strange sitting next to her on my grandparent's couch and seeing her with a big belly, because I had just seen her at the beach last summer. Other than the belly, she hasn't changed much.

Estha isn't the only one that is pregnant. Carrie, my friend from Ally's house, is going to have a baby, too.

*   *   *   *   *

It's my first year in a real high school. I sign up for all honors academic classes, and photography and Junior Reserved Officer Training Corp for electives. I decide I am joining the military after I graduate.

Papa is happy with my decision to join the military, because he says it's the best opportunity to see the world and get paid to do so. I am glad both he and Gramma are proud of me.

Even though things are changing drastically, I feel that they are for the better. I am happy for the first time in a long time. I am able to have friends come to my house. I am able to go places and do normal things with my friends. I live in a house that I am not afraid to go home to – one that I call can truly home. I look forward to walking in the door and seeing Gramma or Papa – even if they are just watching the evening news or a game show – and smelling Gramma's homemade spaghetti sauce.

Best of all, I am allowed to be heard.

Epilogue

Capitalizing the title UNHEARD was intentional, because it represents the things inside of us that are screaming to be heard. I had often asked myself "Why me?" and wondered what was wrong with me as a person, because I had had so many difficulties in many relationships. I hated myself for many years, judging myself harshly for any little mistake that I made, continually finding myself in self-destructive patterns, and wanting to end my life. For years, I chose friends and lovers that did not serve my spiritual well being. Instead, I was choosing what I had known – I had allowed others to bully me, insult me, and treat me with inhumane disrespect. No matter how hard I tried, I didn't see the patterns and heartache that I was causing myself. Acknowledging my mistakes was my first step towards healing. As difficult as it was, I knew that another step towards the healing process was to cut ties with any and all virulent relationships, even if it meant long-term friends and my own family members.

Writing UNHEARD was a great form of therapy for me. Being my own editor forced me to review the patterns in significant relationships throughout my life. It enlightened me in more ways than years of counseling had accomplished. I had finally begun to realize that all of my adult relationships were being replayed from my childhood.

I cannot blame anyone for my own weaknesses, nor can I continue to condemn myself. Alternatively, I can only learn from my experiences and accept them for what they are; it is the only way to move on.

UNHEARD is the first of a series of memoirs in the making. In writing UNHEARD, my intention is to help others who are also struggling with the same demons, with the hope that they may find the healing they need and deserve.

About the Author

Susanna Hartigan is a research journalist living in Florida. She writes poetry, fiction, and nonfiction, and she is the author of several newspaper and magazine articles.

More of Susanna's writing can be viewed on her blog at: http://susannahartigan.blogspot.com

www.ingramcontent.com/pod-product-compliance
Lightning Source LLC
Chambersburg PA
CBHW030939090426
42737CB00007B/483